JEFFREY EISEN, PH.D.

J. B. LIPPINCOTT COMPANY

PHILADELPHIA AND NEW YORK

*To my wife, my daughter,
my mother, and my sister
for their love and caring.*

Copyright © 1978 by Jeffrey Eisen, Ph.D.
All rights reserved
First edition
2 4 6 8 9 7 5 3 1
Printed in the United States of America
Published in association with Diane Harris

U.S. Library of Congress Cataloging in Publication Data

Eisen, Jeffrey.
    Get the right job now!

    Includes index.
    1. Vocational guidiance. I. Title.
HF5381.E49   650'.14   78–11707
ISBN–0–397–01349–3
ISBN–0–397–01311–6(pbk.)

CONTENTS

STAGE ONE: PINPOINTING THE TARGET   **11**
     1. WHERE DO YOU GO FROM HERE?   15
     2. WHAT IS A HEALTHY CAREER?   19
     3. THE RIGHT OCCUPATION   28
     4. THE RIGHT FIELD   41
     5. THE RIGHT COMPANY   46

STAGE TWO: KNOWING THE TARGET   **55**
     6. THE EMPLOYER'S DREAM   57
     7. DESCRIBING THE JOB   63

STAGE THREE: TARGETING YOUR P-IMAGE   **73**
     8. TARGETING YOUR EDUCATION   75
     9. TARGETING YOUR EXPERIENCE   84
   10. TARGETING YOUR SKILLS AND ABILITIES   92
   11. TARGETING YOUR PERSONAL IMAGE, OR HOW
       PEOPLE REALLY GET HIRED   104

STAGE FOUR: PUTTING YOURSELF ACROSS   **115**
   12. RÉSUMÉS THAT PUT YOUR POSITIVE SELF-IMAGE ON PAPER   117
   13. PUTTING YOURSELF ACROSS THROUGH BODY LANGUAGE   131
   14. "SIT DOWN AND TELL ME ABOUT YOURSELF"   147
   15. TRAPS INTERVIEWERS SET   176
   16. NOW THAT THEY WANT YOU   196

SOME ADDITIONAL PROBLEMS YOU MIGHT HAVE   **213**
   17. WOMEN IN A MAN'S WORLD   215
   18. MAKING TOKENISM WORK FOR YOU   239

     INDEX   253

ACKNOWLEDGMENTS

I would like to thank my wife, Laurel, for her ideas, her encouragement, her clarity, and her help in thinking through many of the chapters. I also want to thank Jill Bokar for contributing extensive research and original ideas to the chapter Women in a Man's World and Daniel Beekman for sharing his analyses of the subject in general. My thanks to Lou Sherwood for helping me to target the book to its intended audience. Finally, I would like to thank my students and clients over the years for teaching me much of what I know about job targeting in particular and human nature in general.

STAGE
ONE:
PINPOINTING
THE
TARGET

This book will teach you a new way to get jobs. It is called job targeting. Job targeting will completely change the way you think about your career. Not only will it affect your perception of yourself as an employee, it will also alter your ideas of the way employers think and of what they are looking for when they see you. As a result of job targeting, you will be able to get jobs much more easily—and better jobs, at that. Even more important, you are going to get jobs which will be more fulfilling and which will truly advance your career.

How can job targeting deliver so much? Not by means of magic or a series of tricks, but through solid information and sound techniques. It will teach you to cherish your own needs yet be tough-minded about what employers are and are not looking for. It will teach you invaluable skills: how to research the requirements of the particular jobs you want, how to make good use of your findings, and how to write résumés, handle interviews, and negotiate salary. But most of all, it will show you how to craft an image of yourself that will nearly meet the employer's dream of the perfect employee and that will get you hired.

This image of yourself is at the very heart of the job-targeting approach. I call it your Positive Professional Image or your P-Image. If, in job targeting, the job is your target, your P-Image is your means of reaching the target. Another way of saying it is that it is your P-Image which is being shaped—or targeted.

More needs to be said about this. As you will find out, effective job getting requires you to present yourself in very particular ways at the interview. Exactly what this consists of is the subject of a good part of this book. In brief, you have to come across as a positive, enthusiastic, outgoing person, without any real problems or weaknesses. Above all, you have to qualify for the specific job, and this means presenting yourself in a way slanted to make you seem the ideal candidate for that job.

Most people, when they interview for jobs, sense that they have to sell themselves, but they run into trouble by trying to be too genuine. All of us have mixed feelings about who we are, how we want to relate to other people, and how we want others to relate to us. These feelings get in our way. They bring personal complexities into the job interview that are totally out of place. They also make us unable to present ourselves properly and to manipulate the interviewer.

This is the value of the P-Image. Your P-Image is not yourself. It is a specific projection of yourself created just to get a job, a rewritten version of your history, education, job background, abilities, skills, and even personality crafted to make you as employable as possible. When you use this job-targeting technique, you go into the interview with a new version of yourself.

Your P-Image is something you will work at the way a performer works at an act. You will constantly improve and add to it. As your P-Image becomes more refined and you become more skilled at playing it, you will, of course, get better at getting the jobs you want.

The job-targeting approach has four basic stages. The first

is called Pinpointing the Target. This stage begins with re-evaluation of your project career. It leads to a decision about what types of jobs it would be wisest for you to pursue and then sends you out to locate specific ones.

The second stage of job targeting is called Knowing the Target. In this stage you learn about jobs and employers and about how to research and describe those jobs you want. It is through this knowledge that you will be able to effectively target your P-Image and get these jobs.

The third stage of job targeting is called Targeting Your P-Image. Separate chapters will guide you in targeting your education, your job background, your skills and abilities, and your personal image, until finally all of the aspects of your P-image are covered.

The fourth and last stage of targeting is called Putting Yourself Across. This is the action stage. This stage is concerned with résumé writing, body language for the interviewing situation, talking about yourself, interviewing tricks and strategies, and, finally, closing and negotiating techniques.

This summary of job targeting about sums up the book as well, except that there are two more chapters—one on the special problems women face in getting jobs and the other on the special problems members of minority groups face.

And now, on to the next chapter, where you will begin job targeting with an evaluation of your career and the relationship between its health and your job-getting success.

WHERE
DO YOU GO
FROM HERE?

1

I am going to begin this chapter with a radical statement: If you have come to the end of one job and don't know where to go for the next one, there is something very wrong with your career!

Obviously, there are exceptions to this statement. If you have just finished school; if you are returning to work after raising a family, living abroad, or trying to make it farming in Vermont; or if you are a castaway from a fallen industry, it is more accurate to say you don't yet have a career, or you are changing careers. But in any case, the general sense of what I am saying holds. If you are at the end of one job and don't know where to go for the next one—the problem lies in your career.

Why? Because people who are well established in healthy careers are seldom at a loss for where to go next.

Even when they find themselves at the end of a job, they seldom find themselves at the end of their resources. Their career skills and experiences are in demand and have real value in a defined marketplace. They know successful people in other companies in their field and are known and respected by them in return. They usually know of some openings and have ready access to information about others. And when they apply for these openings, they know how to dress, present themselves, and talk shop.

These people know what they like to do and what they are good at. Finding the next job for them is more a matter of looking around, considering all available options, and choosing those which are best for them than it is a matter of starting from scratch with the classified ads, an attaché case full of résumés, a shine on their shoes, and their hearts in their mouths.

On the other hand, when people who are not established in healthy careers come to the end of a job, they often hit a dead end. They have tried something and it has failed. Whether they have been fired or quit, have been unable to succeed or are uninterested in continuing, whether it was the wrong company, the wrong field, or the wrong kind of work, hardly matters in the long run. The point is that, having tried something that didn't work, they are now at a loss for what to do next.

If this resembles your situation, if you find yourself looking for a job in the uncharted immensity of the employment pages with only vague indications of what you want to do, what you can do, and how to get to be employed doing it, you have a problem. The problem is not that you are out of a job. The problem is that you are not established in a healthy career. The difficulty you are having in finding a job now is just a symptom, and perhaps not even the most serious symptom (although it is probably the most threatening one on a day-to-day level), of your unrecognized career problem.

Actually, you probably experience your lack of career resolution in a number of ways, ways which interfere with your ability to get a job and, most likely, with many other aspects of your life as well.

FINDING YOURSELF

One frequent problem is a feeling that you haven't found yourself. Another problem is a strong sense of restlessness, a dissatisfaction, that keeps one part of you always searching and blocks you from putting all your energy into what you are doing. These negative attitudes prevent you from achieving the success you might otherwise have. And, of course, this in turn tends to discourage and demoralize you, so that you begin to think there is something wrong with you and that you will never find success.

Along with this comes a general anxiety about your life—an urgent feeling that something is wrong and something must be done about it, without your really being able to put a finger on what it is.

On yet another level, you experience a sense of creative frustration. You need an outlet that is interesting, meaningful, and alive for you—one that you care about and can sink your teeth into, that you can really test yourself against and grow with.

You might also experience lack of career involvement as a lack of meaningful connection with the world. Work is one of our principal ways of relating to society and provides many of our social contacts and life interests. If your work is not meaningful, you will experience a lack of connection for which you will be driven to compensate in other ways, perhaps by oversocializing or throwing yourself into leisure pursuits. This will steal energy from your career when you most need to invest it there. In the long run, it can lead to a serious career failure that damages your entire life.

This discussion just touches on the life problems which may come from the failure to establish oneself in a healthy career. These statements may seem exaggerated, but I'll bet that if you are honest with yourself, you will be able to see some of these problems developing to one degree or another even now!

Fortunately, they are not neurotic problems but situational ones, and if the career failures which cause them go away, they will go away too. Career success is something everyone can achieve. But to begin with, you must resolve to develop an appropriate career, not just find another job.

HOW DO YOU START?

O.K. Now you know that the key to both job security and job fulfillment is a healthy career and that you should be aiming at that and not just another job. Good. Now what you want to know is: Just what is a healthy career, and how do you go about getting one?

The first thing to do is stop looking for a job. Why? Because if you keep on looking without first examining your career options, chances are that one of two grave misfortunes will befall you: either you will get a job or you will not. If you do, it will probably turn out to be a dead end like your previous jobs. Nothing that gets in the way of a constructive career hurts like getting stuck in the wrong job. On the other hand, you may not get any job at all, and if that happens you will start to become discouraged and demoralized. This will, of course, put you under tremendous pressure to take the first job to come along, and then you're back to the first problem.

So what should you do? If you are still employed, stay employed until you are ready to get the right job. If you are unemployed and can hold out financially for a while, stay unemployed and do the same thing. If you are unemployed and strapped, find some sort of temporary work to hold you over. But whatever you do, stay free.

Let's take a look at your present career together and determine what it consists of and what its basic problems are.

WHAT IS
A
HEALTHY CAREER?

2

Just what is your career? It is the part of your life that provides you with your livelihood. It began, of course, with your education, and it includes all the jobs you will ever hold. It also covers a wide range of job-related activities. Although some jobs are nine to five, in and out, most higher-level jobs are not. They may affect your social life, the way you dress, the periodicals you read, and even where you live.

THE SIGNS OF A HEALTHY CAREER

ORGANIZATION

If your career is a healthy one, it will have certain unmistakable attributes. First of all, your career will be organized around a more or less well-defined nucleus. It may be a single broad occupational role, such as a salesperson, or it may include both field and occupational roles, such as a dental hygienist or advertising copywriter.

GROWTH

Even established careers grow and sometimes change both fields and roles, but usually there is some coherence in the changes. The person will either stay in the same role but jump fields, like a writer who jumps from a trade publication to public relations, or move to a more suitable or more responsible role within the same field, as does a computer programmer who becomes an account executive.

If your career is a healthy one, it will only change in growth directions, directions which will suit your needs better or give you more status, responsibility, opportunity, and money.

Changes that seem disconnected—for instance, when a person leaves a job in middle management and takes another selling insurance—or that don't progress toward more satisfying or more responsible and remunerative work but show, rather, a history of disconnected, lateral jumps, are signs of an unhealthy career.

FULFILLMENT

Another characteristic of a healthy career is fulfillment. People with healthy careers usually like them. This, of course, is not a hard and fast rule. Many people complain bitterly about their work—often suffering from the stress, the working conditions, and the demands on their time and energy, and even roundly disliking many aspects of the work itself—yet are still deeply satisfied on an essential level.

Different occupations offer different satisfactions, and tasks which meet one person's needs may be unrewarding to another. For instance, you may get your satisfaction sitting at a drafting table designing freeways, happy to endure long hours and confinement in return for the creative satisfaction, while somebody else would go crazy this way.

Still, if your career is a satisfying one, there are certain characteristics you will share with others whose careers are equally satisfying. You will like your work and look forward to it. This does not mean you will like everything about it, but that the core of what you do will be enjoyable. You will also get ego reinforcement from what you do—that is, it will be something which you take pride in doing successfully and which makes you feel more competent.

INVOLVEMENT

Another aspect of a healthy career is involvement. If your career is a healthy one, you will be interested in it and will have an involvement in the field that goes beyond the demands of your own job. You might keep up with trade or technical journals, attend meetings and conventions, be active in professional organizations, and the like. You will also probably find some of your colleagues congenial, and even admirable, and you will probably share common interests with them. On the other hand, if you are really not interested in your work, you will resent having to take time for any outside activities. The only colleagues you will enjoy will be those who are similarly alienated. And you will probably spend happy hours with them over a glass of beer sharing sarcastic evaluations of the company, the boss, the industry, and everyone in it.

SUCCESS

The most telling aspect of a healthy career is success. If your career is healthy, you will be good at what you do. You will do it with relative ease, and you will be successful. Furthermore, this success will not exist only in your own estimation; employers and colleagues will recognize it, and it will be rewarded by advancement, respect, and a certain amount of envy and competitiveness in your colleagues' attitudes toward you. This recognition will frequently extend beyond the company you work for, so that you are known in the industry. Perhaps there will even be other employers who have their eyes on you. Along with this success will usually come a certain degree of job security, since nobody fires a successful employee without very good cause. Finally, if you are successful, you will be earning a better-than-average salary for your position and seniority in the industry.

A HEALTHY COMPANY

There are two more aspects of a healthy career that must not be overlooked. One is relatively easy to remedy, and the other is extremely difficult. .

First of all, you must be working in a healthy, growing company, one that has a future, is expanding, hiring new people, and moving its present employees into jobs which are more responsible and higher paying.

Not all companies are healthy, by a long shot. Every field has companies that are expanding while others are dwindling, with new companies that are trying to break in while old, once-well-established ones are failing. Many things weaken the health of companies: poor management, an antiquated plant, a badly designed or out-of-date product line, poor advertising or sales, a bad reputation . . . the list is long. If you have a fairly good job in an unhealthy company, you may understandably want to hold on to it. You will rationalize this in a variety of ways, hoping that things may get better, wondering whether things would be any different elsewhere, or fearing that you couldn't get an equally good job if you switched.

This is an extremely negative and dangerous way of thinking. Few things are as likely to ground a potentially successful career as the right job in an unhealthy company. It will lead you into a negative, self-protective, constricting frame of mind. You will be fighting to protect your eroding position. And you will still be holding on there years from now, while others who started after you in healthier companies will have forged way ahead.

There is only one thing that a good job in a dying company can do for you, and that is to give you a jumping-off point for a job in a healthier company.

Use it for that!

A HEALTHY INDUSTRY

Of all the things which can ail a company, there is nothing worse than to be in a dying industry. Sometimes a strong company in a dying industry can save itself if it acts in time by branching out into other areas and making use of its plant and its capabilities to capture new worlds. But if it doesn't do that it will soon begin to suffer the attrition endemic to its industry.

Dying industries usually fail slowly, with weak companies failing and strong ones cutting back. Highly qualified employees are continually being cut loose, and many of them continue to hang around, competing fiercely for the few remaining openings in other companies. Don't be one of them!

A LOOK AT YOUR OWN CAREER

At this point, the first step in your appointment with yourself is to take a look at your own career and see if it is a healthy one or not. Of course, nothing is all black or white, and you may find that your career is healthy in some respects and less so in others. Some careers are fine the way they are, some are so unhealthy as to best be changed totally, and most are simply in need of some restructuring and redirecting. The more detailed your understanding of the strengths and weaknesses of your own career, the better you will be able to improve it. For your convenience, the basic points of the last section "The Signs of a Healthy Career" have been distilled into a series of questions. Answer these questions for yourself. If any of them are unclear, reread the relevant discussion on the preceding pages.

THE TWO-MINUTE CAREER QUIZ
that takes some time to think about

1. Is your career organized around a central nucleus consisting of
   a. A given occupational role?
   b. A given industry?
   c. A given occupational role within a given industry?
   d. None of these?

2. Examine the pattern of your major job changes (full-time jobs since graduation). Do these changes show continuity and growth
   a. Of a given role?
   b. In a given industry?
   c. In both role and industry?
   d. None of these?

3. Examine the pattern of your major job changes. Do they show growth
   a. Toward more job satisfaction?
   b. Toward more job reward (salary, title, responsibility, benefits, etc.)?
   c. Both of the above?
   d. Neither of the above?

4. Do you have a sense of satisfaction and self-respect from your work
   a. In your present job?
   b. In your career over the last five years?

5. What is your involvement in your career beyond the demands of your job?
   a. Do you experience a fair number of your colleagues as congenial?
   b. Are you involved in professional organizations?
   c. Do you read professional journals and newspapers?
   d. Are you involved in further study or training?

6. Are you successful
   a. In your own eyes?
   b. In the eyes of colleagues?
   c. In being known in the field beyond your company?

    d. In being well paid considering your seniority, position, company, and industry?

7. Are you in a healthy, growing company with opportunities for advancement?

8. Are you in a healthy, growing field?

WHAT DO YOUR QUIZ RESULTS MEAN?

Now let's take a look at your answers and see what they tell about the health of your career and the ways you might have to revise or redirect it.

Question 1. When your career has no central nucleus, you cannot properly consider it a career, only a succession of jobs. You have yet to discover in what direction you want to go. You should also ask yourself why you haven't settled down. Perhaps you have personality difficulties which make it hard for you to do well in any job and you need counseling. Or perhaps some conflict or confusion about values is preventing you from pursuing the work you would like.

If your career is organized by a given role or occupation, that's fine—if you like your occupation and your needs are satisfied by it. If not, however, consider a change.

If your career is organized around a given industry, consider whether the industry offers you sufficient possibilities for finding satisfying roles and for personal advancement. Again, if it is not, consider a change.

If your career is organized by both role and industry, and you may be in danger of becoming overspecialized and caught in a middle-level dead end, look to make sure there are some viable possibilities ahead for you.

Question 2. If your job changes show no coherent pattern of development, that is an unmistakable sign that you have not yet become established in a career. The pattern that is consistently in a given role, or a given industry, requires that you make sure the role suits you or the industry offers adequate opportunities for advancement. If you are moving along a path of advancement within the same role and the same industry, you are on a very tight (although probably secure) track, so it is important that you are doing something you want to be doing.

Question 3. If the pattern of your job changes shows no growth, you are in a very unhealthy career. You are either in a form of employment without a future or, more likely, you are really misplaced in doing what you do. If you are moving toward more job satisfaction but not more external reward, the external rewards will probably come in time. But if you are moving toward more external rewards but not more job satisfaction, you are in danger of being trapped in work you don't like but which is too well paid to quit.

Question 4. If you don't get a sense of satisfaction and self-respect from your work, you had better find something more congenial to do. Look at chapter 3, The Right Occupation.

Question 5. If you are not involved in your career, it is just a job to you. Sometimes people who are skillful and disciplined, and have outside sources for creative satisfaction, do perfectly well in jobs that are just jobs. Most, however, gradually lose interest and become less effective, often trying to change fields when it is too late.

Question 6. I firmly believe there are no incompetent employees, only misplaced ones. If you are not successful, you are probably in the wrong job. Perhaps you are not receiving recognition and economic rewards but are involved in your work. In this case, you are probably in the right industry, but you have to find a more suitable role within it.

Question 7. If you are not in a healthy, growing industry, find a job in a strong industry, even if you step down in salary and position. Do it now!

Question 8. Finding another job requires total career reorientation. If you are lucky, the roles you are skilled in will transfer to another field, and your task is to locate likely possibilities. If you are unlucky, you will have to reconsider your total range of aptitudes and interests to see what other things you might want to do and could conceivably get to do. Then you must find a way to get to do them.

YOUR CAREER TASKS

Now that you have completed your career quiz, decide what your career tasks are. Do you need to find another job of the same type but in a different company? Should you look for totally different work?

You will have to think about your needs, abilities, and interests for a while to figure out the sort of work that will really satisfy you and take advantage of your strengths. Take some time to do this and, as you proceed, draw up a list of what you consider your career tasks to be.

THE
RIGHT
OCCUPATION

3

As we have seen, getting the right job is essential to a healthy career. Without that, all else is just wishful thinking. But what does the right job mean? Is it almost any job in a large and prosperous corporation? For some people this might be the right answer, but for most it will not be. Is it almost any job in a field you are attracted to, say, television or the resort industry? Again, this might be the answer for some, but not for most. Is it a job (in the sense of an occupational role) which is right for your temperament and training in any company and any field that offers you competitive compensation and advancement opportunities?

The right job ideally optionalizes all the factors of occupation, field, and company. Only then will you be able to enjoy the maximum growth, involvement, satisfaction, and success which will mean a truly healthy and fulfilling career for you.

How does one go about achieving this ideal? First, you must identify the occupations, fields, and companies that might be really right for you. The second thing to do is pinpoint the jobs that exist in these areas. The third step is to get one of these jobs!

Chapter 2, What Is a Healthy Career?, contained a quiz that showed you which aspects of your career are healthy and which need attention. In particular, you learned whether you will need to do something about finding a more appropriate occupation, a better field, or a more suitable company.

Chapters 3, 4, and 5 will help you find the right occupation, the right field, and the right company for you. If you have no problem with one or more of these, feel free to skip the relevant chapter. However, if you have some doubts, you might want to skim the material, at least.

DO YOU HAVE THE RIGHT OCCUPATION?

The most important component of career fulfillment is the right occupation. Most people who have been unable to establish themselves in healthy careers have occupations that are totally wrong for them. They may lack the necessary skills or be displeased by the responsibility level, the working conditions and pressures, or the social milieu. It is possible that these people's jobs are totally unsuited to their temperaments. Some examples: people with gregarious, outgoing personalities who try their hand at computer programming; shy, introverted types who struggle to sell insurance; people who love to work with their hands but are misguidedly employed as bookkeepers; and creative spirits who manage stockrooms.

Not surprisingly, people who are in the wrong occupations are usually in them for the wrong reasons. Either they do not realize what they should be doing or they fail to fulfill their goals. As a result, they motivate themselves to do the wrong jobs through a number of false external factors. They allow themselves to be seduced by prestigious titles and offices, promises of easy work, generous compensations, and the like. They take jobs that will impress their friends and families. Or they opt for locations that boast of "good schools" and "recreational facilities." They do these things instead of asking themselves what is right for them.

People who follow this path of least resistance sometimes

blunder into satisfactory careers, but more frequently they do not. Sometimes they get trapped into careers they hate, but where the money is too good to leave. Other times, they get trapped into careers which are not well paid, but so much time has elapsed that they no longer have any options and so are forced to stay there.

If you are one of these people who has fallen into the wrong occupation, resolve to do something about it now. It will become more difficult in time, not easier.

Choosing an occupation is the most important part of finding the right job for most of us. The phrase "right occupation" describes only the kind of work you are doing, not where you are doing it. For instance, if your occupation is selling, you can sell anything, from textiles to airplanes. You can work for any company and still be a salesman. Furthermore, though aspects of the selling job will vary from company to company, the essence will be very much the same, *i.e.,* you will be selling a product to customers, convincing them that your product meets their needs, and so on. It is this basic core of roles and activities that you should think about when you decide on an occupation.

HOW DO YOU FIND THE RIGHT OCCUPATION?

Some people are lucky. They are drawn to a particular occupation early in their lives. Certain high-reward, prestigious occupations like law, medicine, architecture, journalism, and the arts, as well as romantic callings like aviation and space, some fields of science, and the glamour industries, seem to draw people from childhood. Most of these careers are demanding and competitive, however, which keeps a lot of people out of them.

Other people either find themselves while in school or are fortunate enough to discover a congenial area in their first years of full-time employment. Many, however, never really find a satisfactory occupation. Some of us prepare for something only to find that it doesn't suit us, while others go from job to job, never really liking any, and settling down to something or other out of discouragement or necessity.

Very few of us undertake any serious self-exploration in order to discover what is right for us. Yet self-exploration is not difficult and yields enormous dividends.

The occupation analyzer presented in this chapter will help you find your occupational strengths and priorities. There are two major considerations in determining what occupation you should pursue. One is what you like. And, naturally, the other is what you are good at. The occupation analyzer lists a number of general occupational characteristics. To the right of each characteristic are two columns. Use the first to show whether this is something you like. In the second, indicate if it is something you are good at. As has been done on the sample, mark each column with a plus (+), a zero (o), or a minus (−). A plus in the first column means you like it; in the second column it means you are good at it. A zero in the first column means you neither strongly like nor dislike it; in the second column it means you are neither talented nor untalented at it but could do it competently. A minus in the first column means you actively dislike it; in the second it means you are incapable of doing it competently.

That's all there is to it. Now go ahead and fill yours out.

Occupation Analyzer (Sample 1)

Characteristic	Like	Strength
Working with People	+	o
Working with Paper	o	+
Working with Things	o	—
Information	o	+
Working with Ideas	+	+
Creative Process	+	+
Sales	—	o
Service	—	o
Management	o	o
Working with Numbers	—	o
Working with Words	+	+
Support	—	o
Clerical Work	—	—
Research	+	+
Teaching	o	+
Training	o	+
High Pressure	—	o
Low Pressure	o	o
Long Hours	—	—
Short Hours	+	+
High Involvement	+	+
Low Involvement	—	—
Leader	o	o
Assistant	—	—
Team Member	o	o
Loner	+	+
Working with the Public	o	o
Working with Colleagues Only	o	o
Indoors	o	o
Outdoors	+	+
Physical	+	+
Cerebral	+	+
Nature	+	+
Helping	+	+
Danger	o	o
Physical Difficulty	o	o
Challenge	+	+

Occupation Analyzer

Characteristic	Like	Strength
Working with People		
Working with Paper		
Working with Things		
Information		
Working with Ideas		
Creative Process		
Sales		
Service		
Management		
Working with Numbers		
Working with Words		
Support		
Clerical Work		
Research		
Teaching		
Training		
High Pressure		
Low Pressure		
Long Hours		
Short Hours		
High Involvement		
Low Involvement		
Leader		
Assistant		
Team Member		
Loner		
Working with the Public		
Working with Colleagues Only		
Indoors		
Outdoors		
Physical		
Cerebral		
Nature		
Helping		
Danger		
Physical Difficulty		
Challenge		

Once you have filled out the analyzer, you come to the interesting part. You are going to group all these occupational characteristics according to how much you like them and how competent you are at doing them.

At the top of the list go all characteristics with pluses in both columns (+ +), those things which you both like and are good at.

Next put down all the characteristics which you like and are competent at (+o: a plus in the first column and a zero in the second). Continue in this order:

Zero/pluses (o+), those characteristics you can take or leave but are good at.

Double zeroes (oo), characteristics you can take or leave and can do competently.

Zero/minuses (o –), characteristics you can take or leave but are incompetent at.

Minus/zeros (– o), characteristics you really dislike but could do competently.

And, finally, the double minuses (– –), characteristics you both dislike and are incompetent at.

Now draw heavy lines between each category. Label the top group (+ +) High Priority, the second two (+o and o+) Priority, the next one (oo) Acceptable, the next two (o – and – o) Low Priority, and the last (– –) Reject.

When you are finished, the list should look like Sample 2, but reflect your own likes and strengths rather than those in the sample.

Occupation Analyzer (Sample 2)

High Priority

Working with Words	++
Nature	++
Physical	++
Cerebral	++
Helping	++
Working with Ideas	++
Creative Process	++
Research	++
Short Hours	++
High Involvement	++
Loner	++
Outdoors	++
Challenge	++

Priority

Working with People	+o
Working with Paper	o+
Information	o+
Teaching	o+
Training	o+

Acceptable

Management	o o
Danger	o o
Physical	o o
Physical Difficulty	o o
Low Pressure	o o
Leader	o o
Team Member	o o
Working with the Public	o o
Working with Colleagues Only	o o
Indoors	o o

Low Priority

Working with Things	o –
Sales	– o
Service	– o
Support	– o
Working with Numbers	– o

Reject

Clerical	– –
Long Hours	– –
Low Involvement	– –
Assistant	– –

Before you examine your own list, I'd like you to look at Sample 2 with me.

In the High Priority category are: *working with words, nature, physical, cerebral, helping, working with ideas, creative process, research, short hours, high involvement, loner, outdoors,* and *challenge.*

When I examine these traits, the first thing that comes to mind is that most seem to fit together in the following separate groups, or clusters. Two of them, *loner* and *challenge,* seem to fit in both categories, so I have listed them twice.

Cluster 1. *Working with words, cerebral, working with ideas, creative process, research, short hours, high involvement, loner, challenge.*

Cluster 2. *Nature, physical, outdoors, loner, challenge.*

These two clusters point to two different types of occupations. The first suggests intense, creative, verbal work—probably some sort of writing. The second suggests physical work outdoors. Since most physical outdoor activity does not include writing or other creative verbal work, it is likely that a choice between one or the other will have to be made.

Most people tend to favor verbal work since it offers more prestigious and remunerative jobs. However, this is not necessarily the best thing to do; the whole situation should be considered. For instance, if the person in question was fulfilling his creative verbal needs by writing poetry, he might be far better off with an outdoor physical job than something like working as an advertising copywriter. On the other hand, if he already has a job as a creative writer, he should strongly consider some sort of physical out-of-doors avocation.

Now you are ready to look at your own list. First consider your high priorities (+ +). If everything here seems to go together, you are lucky because they all might be fulfilled in one job. Most people have more than one set of occupational priorities, and some have three or four. Juggle yours around until they fit comfortably into two or more clusters.

Next, consider your priorities, the things you like to do but are only competent at (+o), and the things you feel neutral about but are good at (o+). Look again at Sample 2. In the (+o) set is *working with people*. In the (o+) set we see *working with paper, information, teaching,* and *training.*

The person in this example has no additional priorities here for outdoor physical work but has two more priorities for verbal work: *working with paper* and *information*. This further reinforces the preference for verbal work and suggests that this area should be the occupational choice. A new subcluster of strengths has also shown up: *people, teaching,* and *training*. Such a combination recommends particular verbal occupations like teaching or working with instructional materials. See the way this works?

Now take a look at your own priorities. First, try to fit them into your primary clusters. If some won't fit, see if you can cluster them and look at what they suggest—first considered alongside the primary clusters and then on their own.

GENERATING OCCUPATIONS AND EVALUATING THEM

Now that your occupation analyzer is completed, you have a valuable tool to use in your quest for the right occupation.

STEP 1. Use your priority clusters to generate occupational prospects. Examine your high-priority and priority clusters and think about all the different types of occupations that could fulfill them. Write these down. They will be the beginning of your list of major occupational prospects.

Now see if you can think of any occupations which fulfill two or more clusters. Star these; they are your best prospects.

Your high-priority clusters usually point out your best career options, *i.e.,* verbal/creative, social/high earnings, mechanical /outdoors. The secondary clusters often add a level of definition:

verbal/creative/academic or social/high earnings/selling.

You can consider occupations both on the first, more general level as well as on more specific levels.

Also, it is valuable to show your clusters to friends who might be informed about one or more fields and see what occupations are suggested to them.

STEP 2. Write down all the things you have ever wanted to do, wished you could do, thought you would love, envied other people for, or might be qualified to do by education, training, or experience. Do this in a very free, uncritical way. Don't edit out those things you think are impractical. The time for editing is after your ideas are generated. Let your mind wander back to childhood and the things you wanted to do then. Even if they seem impractical and outlandish, they may hold the seeds for further options.

When you are done, look at your list. Some occupations will seem viable, others absurd, and some, though not viable in themselves, will suggest things which are. Add anything of value to your list.

STEP 3. Look for job listings and descriptions. One good source is the help-wanted pages of a major newspaper like the *New York Times*. Another excellent place to look is in the display want ads for executives in major newspapers. Display ads are particularly good since they describe the jobs. Also look at job descriptions in trade and technical journals.

A number of publications list and describe various sorts of occupations. A key one is the *Dictionary of Occupational Titles*, U.S. Government Printing Office, Washington, D.C. Such books describe most basic occupations and give an extensive breakdown of the sorts of skills which go into them. If you see something anywhere which seems appealing, add it to your list.

STEP 4. Now is the time to edit your list by eliminating entries. First, scrutinize the entire list and cross out any occupation you don't want to do or find totally out of the question for any reason whatsoever.

Reasons for not wanting to do something don't have to be rational, only compelling. If you feel strongly about something, follow your feeling.

On the other hand, if you want to do something but fear it is impossible for some reason, examine your dream job very closely and talk it over with someone who knows the field. Obviously, if you want to be a ballerina and are forty and a beginner, it really is out of the question. However, there might be other dance-related occupations you could go after. If it is the ballet world that appeals to you, you might look for occupations connected with it. If it is creative movement you like, you might consider such things as movement therapy, yoga, or teaching dance to children.

Most fields are more approachable than you might expect. In the last decade, it has become increasingly common for people to have more than one career. There are many people who undertake new careers when they are over forty or in retirement, or after raising a family. The important thing is not to sell yourself—or your situation—short. Decide what you want to do and what is right for you to do, and then worry about whether it is possible or not.

STEP 5. Now use your negative priority cluster to further narrow the field.

Start from the bottom, your low and very low priorities. Consider each occupational possibility on your list and ask yourself if any of them require low or very low priority activities as key tasks. If so put an X by it.

If a given job requires one or more double-minus (− −) tasks among its chief activities, you almost certainly should reject it. If it includes one or more zero-minus (o −) tasks, you should probably reject it as well. The only saving consideration would be if you think you could develop competency at the task in question through special training or counseling.

If a given job has one or more minus-zero (−o) tasks among its chief activities, you should strongly consider rejecting it. However, if other things about the job are attractive enough, and the task in question is not too great a part of the total job, you might consider overriding this negative indication.

Once you note the negatives under each job, it will become clear which are high-priority possibilities and which have too many low-priority drawbacks.

STEP 6. Now compare each occupation on the list to your positive priorities, the + +, +o, and o+ clusters. Look at all the traits in the clusters that would be required by each job and then count the pluses in the traits (+ + equals two) and put the sum of the pluses after each job. This number will give you a rough indication of how well each suits you. Now list the jobs in priority order, starting from the highest number of pluses to the lowest.

STEP 7. At this point, you will have an excellent and compact list of possible and suitable occupations. The next step is to explore these choices further. Start at the top of the list and work your way down.

You may read about the jobs or consult vocational counseling specialists. However, the best sources of information would be people in the occupations whom you can question and, if possible, visit at work to find out what they actually do and what their jobs feel like to you.

Based on what your investigation reveals, you will want to make some final changes on your list, perhaps eliminating some occupations and moving others to a different place. Once you have done this, you will be ready to proceed.

Next, you must consider what fields these occupations are in.

THE
RIGHT
FIELD

4

Most modern fields employ people in virtually every basic occupation. Of course, there are exceptions to this, but as the modern world progresses, the principle becomes more and more true. Almost every major field from packaging to insurance employs people for writing, bookkeeping, advertising, manufacturing, research, engineering, repairing, managing, handling personnel, secretarial duties, health services, interior design, selling, legal services, and so on, for what would be a very long list.

So as you see, deciding what occupation to practice may do very little to narrow down your choice of fields. This is an advantage, since it gives you a great deal of latitude. But it is a disadvantage too; it forces you to focus your career search even more sharply in order to best carry it out. The following pages are designed to give you some help in narrowing down the potentially vast search for a suitable field in which to work.

WHAT ARE MY OPTIONS?

There are two kinds of considerations to keep in mind when examining industries. The first is how you feel about the field itself, what it does, its contribution or detriment to society, the sort of image it has, the people who work in it, its ethics or lack of them, and the like.

The second consideration concerns how well that field meets your career needs. Does it offer adequate employment opportunities for people in your chosen occupation? Will it meet your need for income, security, and advancement? Does it offer working conditions you will enjoy? Does it allow you to live where you want to live?

LIST THE POSSIBILITIES

Both considerations are important. However, before you can even ask the questions they bring up, you need to generate a list of fields you would like to consider.

To begin, list every field that has ever appealed to you for any reason whatsoever. Again, do this in as loose, relaxed, and uncritical way as possible. There will be time to edit later, after the creative generation of possibilities is complete. Give yourself plenty of time to make this list. Don't try to complete it in a day.

Let your memory and imagination have free rein. What fields fascinated you in your childhood? What do you like to do, or fantasize doing, on your vacation? What did you always want to do but gave up as impractical? What sorts of people do you admire? What magazines do you read? What parts of the newspaper do you go to first? The answers to any of these questions may suggest areas that have magic and excitement for you.

Other things you can do: Look at the want ads again to see what fields attract you. Read about various vocations, and decide which seem appealing. Look into reference books and see if any fields described appeal to you.

LEARN MORE ABOUT YOUR CAREER NEEDS

Now ask yourself two sets of questions about your own career needs. The first set is made up of general qualitative questions about the nature of the field. The second deals with more quantitative and practical questions about how well that field will meet your needs for compensation, security, and the like. Answering these questions will make you a better judge of which fields are for you.

Questions to Do with Meaning

1. *Summarize your feelings and beliefs about what function the field you work in should play for society. Which functions are acceptable and which are unacceptable to you?*
2. *What is your image of yourself? What kind of person do you think you are?*
3. *What kinds of surroundings do you see yourself working in?*
4. *What kinds of people do you see yourself working with?*

Questions to Do with Compensation and Working Conditions

1. *What kind of income will you be satisfied with in the next three years?*
2. *What kind of income potential will you be satisfied with in the span of your career?*
3. *How important is job security to you?*
4. *How important to you are various secondary compensations such as:*
   a. *Expense accounts?*
   b. *Stock options, employee profit participation, etc.?*
   c. *Assorted perks such as company cars and travel?*
5. *Where do you want to live and work?*

NARROW DOWN THE POSSIBILITIES

Now that you have a list of industries you might like to work in, and you have clarified a few basic questions for yourself, you are ready to start going down the list and eliminating the unsuitable candidates.

In order to decide whether a possibility is right for you, ask yourself the following questions about it.

1. Does it offer adequate employment opportunities for the occupation you have in mind? (There is no use considering an industry which has no need for the sorts of things you do.)

2. Are there adequate opportunities for advancement? If you are interested in general management, ask whether the occupations through which you might enter the industry lead toward promotion to general executive positions.

3. Does the field offer short- and long-term financial rewards which will continue to satisfy you?

4. Are there sufficient perks?

5. Does the field offer sufficient job security?

6. How are the fringe benefits?

7. Is the field a healthy, growing one which seems to have a good future?

8. How do you feel about the basic social function played by the industry as a whole?

9. Are you in sympathy with the ethics and internal practices that generally prevail in that field?

10. How do you feel about the working conditions you would probably have?

11. Can you live where you would like?

12. How do you feel about the people you would be working with and coming into contact with? Do they interest and excite you, or are you turned off by the prospect of associating with them?

13. Will you be working in congenial surroundings?

14. What image does the field have? Is it one that appeals

to you and fits your own self-image?

15. Are there any foreseeable drawbacks which would prevent you from being happy or successful in this field?

As you look at the fields on your list and ask these questions of them, it will become apparent which are truly good and practical prospects and which should remain subjects for your interest but not considerations for your developing career.

If you don't know the answers to these questions for a field under consideration, you really don't have enough information to make a decision, and I suggest that you research further. If you find yourself reluctant to learn more, it may be a sign that the field is really not that interesting to you.

WHAT FIELDS ARE BEST?

By the time you have finished answering these questions, your list should be considerably shorter. Now I suggest putting it in the order of priorities, with the most attractive field at the top.

How do you go about setting these priorities? There are two criteria. One is how well the field survived your questions. Obviously, not all fields are going to be equally suitable along all lines, and none is likely to be perfect, but some will seem better than others. The other way of ordering them is just to ask yourself which fields have magic for you. Some will simply turn you on. You are going to feel that you really want to work in them, and if it is at all possible you will really stretch to make it happen. If any of these fields survived the basic considerations listed in the previous questions, I would suggest they go to the top of your list.

Now you have your basic list of fields. The next thing is to consider the companies you could work for in these fields.

THE
RIGHT
COMPANY

5

By the time you come to this chapter, you will have focused your career objective on a manageable group of occupations and a fairly small number of fields in which you would like to work. Soon you will be ready to start your search for actual job opportunities, but first I suggest you consider some of the basic differences in companies and see which type would best suit your career needs.

When you are considering the best company for you, there are two basic sets of questions to ask. One concerns *the kind of company it is,* its size, ownership, and the like. The second involves *individual differences between externally similar companies,* for internally, they may be highly dissimilar. Even two major East Coast department stores will differ in organization, personnel policies, advancement opportunities, and general atmosphere.

WHAT KIND OF COMPANY IS IT?

The considerations that follow will help you make an informed choice.

SIZE

Companies vary enormously in size, from multinational conglomerates to those consisting of one person and an answering service. Since this is not a book on self-employment, we will limit our consideration to companies that have at least one employee.

What size company would you like to work for? Many of the advantages and disadvantages of very large and very small ones are obvious. Large companies tend to offer fair advancement practices and excellent advancement opportunities through to the upper middle ranks, a very wide variety of kinds of things (occupations) one can do, excellent benefits, and excellent security. On the other hand, they may be highly anonymous. It is almost impossible to get a sense of the large company as a whole. You may not be able to identify with the organization or estimate the value of your work and its place in the whole effort. People in large companies tend to feel that what they do hardly matters.

In small companies, the situation is reversed. It is easy to see the results of your work—in fact, a large part of the success or failure of the company may visibly rest on your efforts. You are able to identify with the company and to feel important. You know many, and sometimes even all, other employees. On the other hand, advancement opportunities may be extremely limited. Your promotion might have to wait until someone else leaves or the company expands in your area. Job definitions seem to be much looser, and you may find yourself overextended and even overworked. Benefits tend to be less good. Security is probably more precarious; you may find yourself at the mercy of one person for recognition, security, and advancement—so you and that person had better get along.

Of course, between these extremes are an infinite number of variations, and one of these is probably right for you. My suggestion is simply to think about company size and get some sense of what you want and don't want.

OWNERSHIP

Ownership is a further indication of the sort of company you are dealing with. Companies are owned in many different ways. The basic categories of ownership we will consider here are: corporate, private, and nonprofit, with a look at government agencies and professional companies.

CORPORATIONS. Any business may be incorporated, from a Ma and Pa grocery to a multinational conglomerate. But we are concerned only with corporations that are publicly held or large enough to put ownership in the hands of a number of people of different opinions, and management in the hands of professional managers.

Many of our previous considerations pertaining to size hold here as well. Major corporations are large companies, and they usually are not controlled on a minute level by one sometimes highly idiosyncratic person. Their procedures tend to be more standardized, advancement opportunities are more open and equable, and their policies more consistent and fair. The salaries they offer are more representative of the field. And their employee benefits are likely to be more complete. On the other hand, all the drawbacks of large companies hold equally well: anonymity, difficulty of seeing the effects of one's work, and often an atmosphere lacking in creative vitality—essentially, a lot of people holding down their jobs, covering themselves, and passing the buck.

PRIVATELY OWNED COMPANIES. By privately owned companies we mean those owned by individuals and partnerships, and small corporations which are controlled by one or two people. What has been said earlier concerning small companies usually holds true here. Privately owned companies tend to be underfinanced and less well established. They work harder than corporations to maximize profits and minimize expenses. As an employee, you are a potential means of maximizing profits (by maximizing your productivity) and definitely a means of minimizing expenses, by keeping your salary and other compensations as low as possible.

Privately owned companies are also subject to the whims of their owners, so working for them can range from marvelous to horrendous. Either way, the situation will be much less reliable and standardized than what prevails in a major corporation.

Another characteristic of privately owned companies is that there may be no room at the top and very little room near the top. In such a situation, the boss, and perhaps his son, have all the major executive responsibility and glean all the profit. They will probably not advance anyone past an area of moderate earnings, although they will usually try to get as much work as possible out of their employees.

Even when conditions are at their worst, employment in a privately owned company is often an excellent way to gain experience in a field, since you see much more of the whole picture and get to do more things than you would in a relatively circumscribed job in a large company. This type of company would be an excellent place to break into a field if you are an enterprising person who plans to stay only for a year or two and then move on.

NONPROFIT COMPANIES. This category refers to companies financed in such a way that the need to make a profit is not a primary motivation. Under this heading go all sorts of nonprofit foundations, museums, charities, and religious groups. These are often extremely pleasant places to work. They tend to be more genteel, gracious, and idealistic than profit-oriented organizations and often enjoy extremely pleasant and leisurely working conditions. Of course, they are usually less competitive internally as well as externally, though this is by no means always true. One of their drawbacks in this respect is that they may employ influential people whose motivation for being there is not usually financial. For that reason they may be even more involved with ego power drives and games than employees of profit-oriented companies and therefore are harder to get along with.

A nonprofit company tends to undertake many kinds of activities. Among these are (1) the company's primary function or raison d'être (distributing grants, educating people in the hazards of food additives, or whatever); (2) doing whatever is necessary in order to earn money, be this grantsmanship, soliciting contributions, or something else; (3) usually a substantial amount of public relations-oriented work; and (4) general administrative and clerical work.

Two of these activities have a great influence on the nature of the company: the primary function and what the company does to earn money. The primary function of a nonprofit organization is naturally the prime determinant of what the company is like —a listener-sponsored radio station will be very different from a poverty law foundation. If you keep this in mind, you will be able to make a reasonable estimate of the kind of company you are likely to find.

The second determinant, what the company has to do to make its living, is more subtle. Some nonprofit companies are set up by monied interests to carry on specific programs. These are extremely secure and totally beholden to their benefactors. Most, however, are set up by people who realize they must raise funds in order to do what they are doing.

Both the way these funds are raised and how successfully they are being raised will affect the internal workings of the company. If funds are raised primarily through grants, the company is answerable to the granting agency and is subject to many levels of review and inspection, both external and internal. If the organization appeals directly to individual public contribution, it is more protected internally but must worry about its image and public relations. Perhaps the most autonomous and most secure of such companies are those that sell a product or a service but operate on a no-profit charter. However, these companies are often closest to profit-making outfits in operation.

Nonprofit companies offer many benefits if you can get a suitable job in one, but they have disadvantages as well. Salaries tend to be considerably lower, especially in the upper echelons. Standards of professionalism are also often lower without the spur of competition. What's more, when the person who has worked in a nonprofit company decides to switch to a profit-making firm, he often finds that his experience is not fully respected and that the lower salary he has received is a hindrance in getting compensation appropriate to the level of his job.

GOVERNMENT AGENCIES. Government agencies vary. They may be anything from dens of apathy, ineptitude, and surliness like the unemployment bureau to high-level state and federal agencies which set and implement policy. Government agencies tend to be manned by civil service employees and administered by political appointees. This means that the people who do the work are for the most part holding down sinecures, so they often do not try very hard and may behave unprofessionally, while the people who run the agencies are public or potentially public figures whose main concerns are image and avoiding negative publicity. With notable exceptions, government agencies tend to be bureaucratic, noncompetitive, stifling places to work, where the salaries are modest but the security and benefits are excellent. The people who make a career of working in them seem to complain a lot and dress poorly.

PROFESSIONAL COMPANIES. Professional companies consist of groups of professionals like accountants or lawyers who form a firm. They offer essentially two types of positions—professional-associate and clerical-secretarial. As places for clerical-secretarial jobs, they are often excellent, offering good salaries and working conditions and pleasant surroundings. If you are a professional, you can bring more expertise than I to bear on the question of whether they are good places for you to pursue your career.

WHAT INDIVIDUAL DIFFERENCES EXIST
BETWEEN COMPANIES?

As I said before, even companies in the same category are usually extremely dissimilar internally. Some of the factors which differentiate them clearly make one company more desirable than another, while other factors are simply a matter of preference, such as competitiveness and pace.

Some companies have an essentially cooperative atmosphere, emphasize group effort, and are fairly secure places to be. While there are occasional big pushes, they are done in a supportive and cooperative atmosphere. Other companies emphasize the every-man-for-himself approach, everyone constantly struggling to outshine and climb onto the shoulder of another, with a mass of infighting and endless emergencies and crises. If they don't spit you out in two years, ten years in these companies can leave you with an ulcer, rich, or both. There are people who love places like this, and others who can't stand them. Make up your own mind.

Some companies are stuffy, some fashionable, some dowdy, some casual, some hip. It often has a lot to do with what line they are in and where they are—but variations do exist. Corporate law firms are extremely formal; theatrical law firms are fashionable. New York publishers wear suits and ties; L.A. publishers, sport shirts and slacks, but expensive ones. Again, find a place where you will be comfortable.

Another important area is that of ethics, both internal and external. Internal ethics involves the way the company treats its own people, while external ethics applies to its dealings with the people it makes its living from and its competitors. Usually, they are related—that is, companies which are unethical or highly opportunistic on one level tend to behave similarly at all levels.

Unethical or highly opportunistic companies that really don't care what effects their operations have on their customers, their employees, or the world they live in are bad places to be. Working in them makes you an accomplice, and this cannot help but make you feel badly about yourself. It may even profoundly affect your entire life for the worse. It is also likely that sooner or later the company will treat you as ruthlessly as they do everyone else. On the other hand, they are usually places where you can make a lot of money. The decision is yours.

Yet another area is the company's attitude about time. In some companies you work from nine to five with a twelve-to-one lunch break, and that is that. In other companies, your work is the important thing, and if you come in at ten, leave at four or six thirty, or take a long lunch, nobody pays much attention—that is, providing you get a lot of high-level work done. Companies like this also frequently expect similar flexibility on their behalf, so you should be prepared to work Saturdays and evenings on occasion and even for a weekend or two if the pinch is on. If you are an executive, you should not expect to get paid extra for this overtime.

This brings me naturally to the last topic I want to discuss here. Some companies demand extremely high involvement. The people who run the company live for their work, and unless you are on a clerical level (and sometimes even if you are) they expect you to do the same. Overtime, weekends, superhuman efforts to meet deadlines, and competitive fervor are the rule rather than the exception. Everybody works very hard and is very involved emotionally. They expect you to be the same. If you are not, it will be noticed and resented, and you won't last long. On the other hand, the work is often exciting and fulfilling, success is the thing, camaraderie is high, formality is almost nonexistent, and rewards can be excellent. Highly creative companies like advertising agencies, magazines, and fashion houses fall into this category.

Other companies require extremely low involvement. The work is done more or less competently at a leisurely pace, and everyone from the boss down goes home at five o'clock and takes vacations on schedule. The work is fairly cut and dried, and the company's earnings are stable and well established. Places like insurance companies and wholesalers are like this. They are usually places with modest salaries and benefits and are really suitable only for people who have strong outside interests and involvements and want work as a means of supporting their lives, not as a center for them.

Of course, there are many other characteristic differences between companies. But they are too many and too idiosyncratic to discuss here. Once you make some basic decisions about the sort of company you want to work for, you will have to base others on the particular company itself. So if you are considering a job offer, especially if you are choosing between more than one offer, see if you can spend some time in the companies themselves, talking to people and observing the way things are done before you come to a firm decision.

STAGE
TWO:
KNOWING
THE
TARGET

You have now finished the first stage of targeting. You have thought about your career, chosen your potential targets, and made a list of jobs and fields you would like to pursue. Now we proceed to the second stage: Knowing the target. At this point you must become intimately familiar with the requirements of the jobs you are aiming at.

It is important to be as clear and complete as possible in your study of the target. We will go through a number of basic steps to achieve this.

To begin with, you must familiarize yourself with the Employer's Dream. This is a description of all concerns, biases, and demands common to employers in general. To realize that the Employer's Dream exists and to accept it is, in a sense, to lose your innocence. No longer will you be able to fantasize that the employer is the good parent who will recognize, nurture, and reward you. Now you will see him as the focal point of a constellation of economic and organizational forces and problems which he is

55

trying to solve by hiring the appropriate person. Once you accept the Employer's Dream, you accept the employer for what he is and not what you wish him to be. You must try to meet his requirements and thereby meet your own.

The Employer's Dream is your basic reference, and all your efforts to get the job are conceived with this in mind. However, individual employers, naturally, have individual requirements. You must have a very good idea of what these particular requirements are if you want to do really fine pinpoint targeting—the kind of targeting which gets top jobs.

For this reason, we go through the process of describing all requirements of each job or job class which truly interests us. This is not an easy process because it requires time, attention to detail, and, to really do it right, research. You may have a tendency to take shortcuts or skip this task entirely, rationalizing that it requires too much time for a job you might not get anyway. However, when you think about it further, you will realize that any job you are not sufficiently interested in to spend a few hours of research and thought on is probably not worth spending a large part of your life working at. The jobs you really want will hold your attention for a little research. Besides, since jobs in a given class are similar to one another in many ways, the time you spend studying them will not be wasted. To the contrary, it will serve to make you a more skillful and successful targeter.

The descriptions you work up for each job will include: the educational background required, the experience expected of you, the abilities and skills called for, and the sort of personal image the employer will be looking for.

Once this material is researched and you have the description before you, you will be able to proceed to the next stage of targeting with great certainty. This is the stage of actually tailoring your P-Image to the job.

THE EMPLOYER'S DREAM

6

Every employer has a dream of the perfect employee, and chances are you are not it. This is nothing to be upset about, because the average employer's dream is not a very wonderful thing to be from any viewpoint but his; furthermore, it includes many elements so incompatible that they probably cannot be reconciled in any real person. Still, in this world it is rarely enough just to be you, and for the purpose of getting a job it is almost never enough. So I suggest that you familiarize yourself with the concept of the Employer's Dream.

The Employer's Dream, as set forth here, is a general statement. It represents not the desires of any one employer but, rather, a sort of composite of needs which all employers feel are imposed on them simply by the conditions of doing business. It is more an economically determined description than a personal one. Furthermore, no two employers have exactly the same dream. Each has his own version composed of the requirements of the job in question, the needs of the particular business and of the industry as a whole, regional mores, and any personal biases.

Whenever an employer interviews you, he will have this dream in the back of his mind, and he will be comparing you to it. If you conform substantially, and your formal qualifications are suitable, you will be in a good competitive position to get the job. If you don't conform, you certainly won't get it, no matter how well qualified you are. (The only exception to this, and even this is partial, is the case of a person who is highly qualified at a very specialized skill which is greatly in demand. But such a person is not likely to be needing this book.)

Successful application of many of the techniques taught in this book requires you to be familiar with the Employer's Dream, so study it well and think about it.

WHAT IS THE EMPLOYER'S DREAM?

Every time an employer interviews you, he will be asking himself five basic questions:

1. Will you be able to do a good job? *This is the question of* ability.
2. Will you fit in? *This is the question of* suitability.
3. Will you remain with the company and work well there? *This is the question of* stability.
4. Will he make money out of you? *This is the question of* profitability.
5. Are you the sort of person he wants to be associated with? *This is the question of* desirability.

These are logical questions for employers to be asking themselves about you, and up to this point I have no fault to find with them. However, within each question are many concerns—some fair and justified, others arbitrary and discriminatory. These basic concerns of the Employer's Dream are listed according to the categories of ability, suitability, stability, profitability, and desirability. You will probably notice that some listed under one heading might just as easily go under another. This is the result of a partial overlapping of categories. Don't worry about it.

I. ABILITY. Will you be able to do a good job? The employer will be looking for:

1. *Someone of suitable education, training, and experience. (This is a matter of formal qualifications.)*
2. *Someone whose background suggests a lifetime of preparation for this particular job.*
3. *Someone who is intelligent.*
4. *Someone who is energetic.*
5. *Someone who is competent.*
6. *Someone who is realistic and has common sense and good judgment.*
7. *Someone who can follow orders accurately and does not bring an attitude of resentment to dealing with superiors.*
8. *Someone who can manage others and give orders without discomfort and without creating resentment.*
9. *Someone who can work independently.*
10. *Someone who is able to admit having made a mistake and learn from it, but who doesn't make many mistakes.*
11. *Someone with a record of success in other related jobs.*

II. SUITABILITY. Will you fit in? The employer will be looking for:

1. *Someone who will fit into the company's social structure.*
2. *Someone who is courteous and tactful.*
3. *Someone who is cooperative.*
4. *Someone who gets along well with peers, subordinates, and superiors.*
5. *Someone who works well on a team.*
6. *Someone who can both assume and share responsibility.*
7. *Someone who is not a troublemaker, organizer, or malcontent.*

8. *Women who maintain the traditional feminine role, but in a way that is consonant with appropriately assertive job performance.*

III. STABILITY. Will you remain in the company and have a satisfactory attitude toward your work? The employer will be looking for:

1. *Someone who will stay in the business and move up in it so that the effort invested in employee training will come back to the business instead of being lost.*

2. *Someone who is not overqualified.*

3. *Someone who does not have a record of frequent job changes.*

4. *Women who are not likely to leave in order to get married and have children.*

5. *Someone who has been, and preferably still is, successfully employed.*

6. *Someone who will identify with the company and put its interests first.*

7. *Someone whose educational and job backgrounds are conventional and show a coherent and orderly progression to the present position.*

8. *Someone who will be ambitious to succeed in the job, but not to the extent of putting personal ambition above the interests of the company.*

9. *Someone who will bring creativity and initiative to the job, but who will not be dissatisfied with its limitations, no matter how arbitrary.*

10. *Someone who follows through on assignments and responsibilities.*

11. *Someone who has already found himself or herself and*

knows that what he or she wants is in accord with the possibilities of the job.

12. *Someone with personal stability.*

13. *Someone who is not neurotic and is not subject to moods, depressions, anxiety attacks, loss of temper, compulsiveness, or oversensitivity to criticism.*

IV. PROFITABILITY. Will he make money from you? The employer will be looking for:

1. *Someone fully trained and qualified in relation to the job and salary level.*

2. *Someone who brings new knowledge and skills to the company.*

3. *Someone with a proven history of success in making profitable innovations for other firms.*

4. *Someone who brings valuable outside connections, customers, or clients.*

5. *Someone he expects to make money for the firm.*

6. *Someone with creativity.*

7. *Someone hard-driving and aggressive.*

8. *Someone who is flexible and willing to do work outside the basic job requirements, if so requested.*

9. *Someone who is not afraid of hard work and long hours.*

10. *Someone with modest expectations of remuneration.*

11. *Someone who can be exploited.*

12. *Someone in good health.*

13. *Someone young in relation to the job level and never, except in top positions, much over forty.*

V. DESIRABILITY. Are you the sort of person he wants to be associated with? The employer will be looking for:

1. *Someone who is likable.*

2. *Someone who is impressive, but who doesn't make him feel inferior.*

3. *Someone who has gone to prestige schools and has worked for prestige companies.*

4. *Someone who is fairly middle-of-the-road politically.*

5. *Someone who is socially conventional.*

6. *Someone with whom he feels comfortable.*

7. *Someone he feels can be trusted.*

8. *Someone who will make a good impression on others.*

9. *Someone who is attractive and well dressed in an accepted fashion.*

10. *Someone with energy and vitality.*

11. *White Anglo-Saxons or other whites with an Anglo-Saxon manner and appearance—unless it is a firm with minority ownership.*

12. *Non-whites who speak, dress, and behave in a way which resembles white Anglo-Saxons in manner, and who do not share any militant attitudes that might prevail in their ethnic group.*

DESCRIBING
THE
JOB
7

Now describe the jobs you will be applying for as a preparation for targeting your P-Image toward them.

CHECK THE EMPLOYER'S DREAM

The Employer's Dream forms the first part of any job description. In fact, it is so much a part of the description that it is not actually included in it, it is just understood to be operative. However, there is one circumstance in which you should refer to the Employer's Dream in your job description, that is when you encounter a significant exception to it.

For example, item II-8 of the Employer's Dream under Suitability calls for "Women who maintain the traditional feminine role, but in a way that is consonant with appropriately assertive job performance."

Now, however, let us say that you are a woman applying for a job in a feminist organization—say, *Ms. Magazine* or a woman's counseling center. Clearly, that peculiar combination of the traditional feminine role and managerial assertiveness would not be necessary here. In fact, it might easily be resented. A more straightforward and feminist image would be far more effective when applying for this kind of non-mainstream job.

The first step of describing a job, then, is to note any exceptions to the Employer's Dream. Most of the time, however, you will find the Employer's Dream to be an extremely reliable guide with few significant exceptions. Use it, and it will serve you well.

DESCRIBE THE JOB ITSELF

Next, describe the job itself in detail. Give its title, then list all its functions. Be complete and specific. If you can, list whom you will be working for and what division you will be in. Of course, you won't know this prior to your first interview, but one or two meetings should provide you with much of this information. In the meantime, the blank spots in your description can guide you toward finding out what you need to know. If you don't know a job well enough to describe it, find out more about it. The more you know about the job you are applying for, the better you will be able to target your P-Image and your campaign toward getting it.

LIST THE BASIC REQUIREMENTS

EDUCATIONAL REQUIREMENTS. After describing the job itself, list its educational requirements. Start with explicit requirements: the amount of education or equivalent experience, required specializations, special training, and the like. This will be easy, since the information will be either part of the job description or, at least, readily available.

Next, describe the implicit requirements. Most employers won't admit any exist, but usually there are some—for instance, the sort of schools they respect and the majors they will accept. Employers also vary in their demand for prestige factors such as Ivy League schools, special grants, honors, and endorsements by famous faculty. And, of course, some employers look at social achievements, particularly for jobs that require a public image. The graduates they are interested in were successful athletes, held class office, or belonged to top fraternities.

You can save yourself a lot of time and unnecessary discouragement if you get these requirements down. Then you can simply avoid pursuing jobs from which you will be excluded before you have even begun to interview. You can also strengthen your application for those jobs where you stand a chance.

ABILITIES AND SKILLS. All jobs require some general abilities; some may also ask for highly technical or specialized skills. It is important to recognize the abilities and skills required by the job you are applying for so that you are able to assure the employer that you have them.

General abilities range from the elemental ones taken for granted in someone on your educational level (such as the ability to follow procedures) to those that are not possessed equally by every educated person (such as the ability to write clear prose or to do basic math), and to other skills which, though still relatively unspecialized, may be specific to certain business environments, (like the ability to manage others, work in groups, follow orders, and handle correspondence). If any one of these more or less general abilities is important for the job in question, note it and be prepared to emphasize it on the interview.

Specific skills are those required only for particular specialized jobs. They are usually serious prerequisites requiring previous training or experience. Occasionally an employer will give someone with demonstrated aptitude and a related background a chance to acquire a specific skill, but usually you will be expected to come to the job already equipped with it. If your newly emergent job priorities point you toward an area which calls for skills you don't possess in sufficient degree, be prepared either to acquire those skills or to abandon the possibility of such a job.

RESEARCH THE JOB

Most of the time, when you first apply for a job, you really won't have much more information than what you have gotten from the classified pages or, at best, from a display ad of about one hundred words. Other times you may hear of a job through an agency or through somebody who knows somebody, and then your information is likely to be scanty, third hand, and inaccurate. Yet proper targeting requires accurate information.

The only way to deal with this problem is to research the job. This may sound like a difficult task at first, even one you are unwilling to do, but keep in mind that applying for a job is in itself difficult, time consuming, and emotionally taxing. It is made even more difficult by a lack of accurate information.

Researching a job, though it requires more work in the beginning, greatly lessens your efforts in the long run. That is, it saves you from pursuing jobs that you either couldn't get or wouldn't want, and it enhances your chances of getting the job you do want. Not only that, but the very process of researching enhances the interview procedure. The process of familiarizing yourself with company operations and of "interviewing" the interviewer shows you in a positive light as a responsible, energetic candidate who is only interested in the right job and not in any job that is available.

Following are the basic stages in researching a job opportunity.

USE THE TELEPHONE

Be frank about it. You want to find out as much as possible about the job, the company, and the sort of person the company is looking for before you even come in for the first interview. After all, why should you or anybody else waste their time? After you get all that you can from the interviewer by telephone, ask if there is anyone else he would recommend your talking to. By the time you come in you will be well armed with information, and your potential employer will be happily forewarned that a real go-getter is on the way.

LOOK UP THE COMPANY

Find out as much as you can about the company—its activities, size, financial strength, standing in the industry, future plans, and problems. Possible sources for this are its own publications, professional publications, newspapers, and magazine articles. If it is a major company, contact other people you might know in the industry, and any agencies or organizations which might know about it.

INTERVIEW THE INTERVIEWER

Once the interviewing has actually begun, it becomes easier to find things out. You have the interviewer to question. And if the first interview goes well, you can probably gain access to other people in the company.

Of course, if you are fairly sure you want the job, the main information you are after concerns the sort of person the company is looking for and the kinds of qualifications they will expect. However, you must not let the employer suspect that this is your real interest. Instead, present yourself as someone who wants to know as much as possible about the company and the job, so that you can decide whether it's right for you.

It is best to carry out the interview as if this premise were true, because you will learn much more about the job that way. Among other things, you will find that some companies seem far less attractive when seen up close and others seem far more so.

There are a number of other uses for the information you can get by investigating the company at the interview. For instance, you will start to see what some of the company's problems are and get a better view of its operations; and perhaps you can meet some other executives. If you are smart, you will turn all this to your advantage. With more knowledge about the company's operations and problems, you can talk specifically about the role you might play, if hired, and even begin to suggest some strategies and solutions. Short of this, your merely being able to talk about the company from the inside will give the interviewer the impression that you are already part of it. Referring to conversations with people you have met will further this impression. Furthermore, if some of the people you meet like you, they might speak up in your favor.

Also remember that the interviewer is always anxious about hiring someone who won't fit in. If he sees that you are able to find your way around without ruffling anyone's feathers, this will further reassure him that you are a safe choice.

There is yet another benefit which can be squeezed from this process of interviewing the interviewer: gaining control over the interview. In trying to find things out, you will, of course, be mentally formulating a number of questions to ask the interviewer. Every time you ask one of these questions, it will have the effect of changing the subject from the previous topic to whatever you asked about.

There are times in any interview when changing the subject like this is a very desirable thing to do. One time, of course, will be when you are in a tight spot and want to get the interviewer off a given line of questioning as quickly as possible. Another time might be when you are using closing techniques like "overcoming objections." Let us say that you have just tried to overcome his objection to your lack of direct-mail experience. You might say something like, "That is true, but as you know, I am extremely skilled in media advertising. When I began in that field three years ago, I had no advertising background at all, so I'm sure I won't have any trouble picking up direct mail just as quickly."

Now that you have dealt with this objection, you don't want

him to dwell on it and find more objections. You want to get him on to something else, feeling that his objection is invalid. This is a good time to ask an investigative question—something to take his mind off his objection, make him a little defensive about the merits of his company, and remind him what a demanding applicant you are and how lucky he would be to persuade you to join his company.

So don't stint time and effort when it comes to researching the jobs you are interested in. Good research will save you far more time and effort than it will cost you.

WHAT ARE THE PERSONAL REQUIREMENTS?

Many employers are not only looking for someone with the appropriate education, job experience, and abilities, they are looking for a certain kind of person as well, one who fits an image they have in mind.

Most images employers are looking for come under the Employer's Dream, but some do not. In fact, employers might be put into two categories: equal opportunity employers and "our kind" employers. Equal opportunity employers hire people primarily on merit (or at least on qualifications). They expect employees to be appropriately dressed, speak good English, and know how to behave themselves correctly. Beyond that, they are mostly concerned with how well a person can do the job. "Our kind" employers, on the other hand, though equally concerned with qualifications and ability, only consider those they perceive as being the right kind of person.

"Our kind" employers are a various lot and, of course, seek various kinds of people, so the first principle is not to try to fit in with all of them. It is impossible.

The "our kind" companies most people will want to break into will be those with a prestige image that is upper-class, WASP, old-money, Ivy League. This encompasses a good number of established, prestigious, high-income firms. However, there are also many highly idiosyncratic "our kind" employers with extremely different standards: creative, artistic, or theatrical employers, firms with ethnic management, or organizations involved with altruistic issues and social causes, for example. Companies and organizations like these typically discriminate in favor of people they identify with. If you don't happen to fit in with their image, getting hired by them can be just as difficult as getting into an old-money firm.

If you would like to be hired by an "our kind" company that you don't fit into already, you will have to be willing to remake your personal image. This may include changing the way you dress, speak, and eat, the things you read and talk about, your attitudes, opinions, and politics, and so on. For many people this is an extremely unpleasant option, but if the job you want calls for it, it is what you will have to do.

When describing the personal-image requirement of a job you are interested in, go through the following procedure. First, ask yourself if it deviates significantly from the Employer's Dream, and if it does, note just how. Then ask yourself what particular bias it has. Is it a company with an upper-class WASP image? If so, consider whether it is possible for you to be employed by such a company. Some actually require a social background of you. Others only ask that you look and act as if you have that background. Forget the first kind unless you qualify. If the company is the second kind, observe everything you can about the people employed there and be prepared to mimic them.

If you are interested in a more idiosyncratic company, ask yourself just what their bias is. Are they looking for creative types, militant types, real people, aggressive salespeople capable of cutting throats as well as deals? Decide what their type really consists of, and play it to the best of your ability.

Then, regardless of the kind of company it is, move on to the specifics. How do people there dress, talk, and behave, and what sort of attitudes, opinions, and politics do they espouse?

Where do they go for lunch, and what sorts of things are they interested in outside of work? Describe everything as carefully as possible. The more you know, the better your chance of getting the job.

STAGE THREE: TARGETING YOUR P-IMAGE

Now you have learned the proper way to describe a job. It is best to go through this process for each job that has your sincere interest. With the description before you, you will have a specific and detailed account of what the job consists of and how you will have to be perceived by the employer if you are to get it. Armed with this information, you can proceed to tailor your P-Image to the job in mind with skill and accuracy. It is for this reason that the job description is the cornerstone of the whole targeting process. Lay the cornerstone carefully.

TARGETING
YOUR
EDUCATION
8

If you have ten to twenty years of job experience in related industries, it's not going to matter to your prospective employer whether your college major was in a related field or what your average was at graduation. Your job record will have superseded your educational record. About the only thing that might be noted, and that only by some employers, is what college you went to and whether you were a famous athlete or not.

On the other hand, you may just be graduating from college, technical school, law school, or whatever and are knocking on the doors of the real world for your first job. In this case, you might find employers paying quite a lot of attention to what school you went to, what your major was, how good your grades were, and what you did there. After all, what else tangible do you have to offer?

Furthermore, the less clear you are on what you want to do and the less prepared you are for any particular kind of job, the more your educational background will mean. For instance, if you walk into the average urban employment agency with no more than a degree in something like literature or philosophy and a desire for interesting, meaningful work, not only will your welcome not be encouraging, it may be downright rude. You will find

only the least appealing jobs offered to you, and these will probably require you to do something you will not consider. Although
there are interesting jobs open to people with "impractical" degrees, they are not the kind handed out by employment agencies
to any bright new graduate who wanders in off the street. It will
require initiative to locate them and skill to get them against a
competitive field. And that means targeting.

Another thing to consider is that employers vary greatly in
how much weight they put on your educational background.
Professional, scientific, and technical employers, of course, put a
great deal of importance on this, even after you have been working in the field for a number of years. Large corporate employers,
particularly those who are working through personnel departments, also will pay a fair amount of attention to your education
if you are a new graduate. Prestige-minded "our kind" companies
pay attention to the school you went to, if not how well you did
there. Beyond that, it is a highly idiosyncratic kind of thing. Many
employers go almost completely on intuition in hiring. They are
far more concerned with how they feel about you, whether you
seem bright and personable, and whether they like you than with
what your educational background was.

If there are any guiding principles, they seem to be these:
jobs that require you to have professional, semiprofessional, scientific, or technical skills of the sort you would learn in school are
most concerned with your education. Next come people who are
hiring you to work for somebody else—for instance, a personnel
department that is hiring you as a management trainee. Their
intuition is largely irrelevant since you won't be working directly
for them, and if they make a mistake they will have to answer to
somebody else for it. They tend to cover themselves by paying
attention to formalities. On the other hand, employers who are
hiring you to work for them directly, particularly in areas where
you will be getting your basic training on the job, tend to pay far
less attention to formal qualifications and far more to how they
feel about you.

LOOK AT YOUR EDUCATIONAL BACKGROUND

The first practical step in targeting your education is to write out your educational background and look at it from the employer's point of view. Start with high school, if it was a prestigious one. If not, start with your higher education, then proceed through your whole educational background, including summer programs, years abroad, extracurriculars, and the like. Also, include anything else you did of significance during your school years.

A good way to work is with two columns, one to give a chronological outline, the other to comment on what you want to emphasize. Emphasize anything worth emphasizing: noted professors, offices held, extracurricular distinctions, and so on.

Once you have done this, work on it with an eye to three things: apparent directions, strengths, and weaknesses.

KNOW YOUR APPARENT DIRECTIONS

An apparent direction is any cluster of educational achievements and experiences which suggest preparation for a given type of work. For instance, a place on the debating team and a social science major suggest an apparent direction toward public service or politics. An award-winning science project and a biology major suggest an apparent direction toward some field of science or environmental management. Things like hobbies also often align with more formal educational experiences to reinforce apparent directions.

Why is this important? Some people decide what they want to do with their lives very early on, and they prepare for it throughout school. But a surprising number of us actually fail to recognize and value our own interests in terms of a possible career. The world is full of people with a passionate interest in music or collecting rocks who made unhappy careers in business simply because they failed to value their interests.

Apparent directions are your way of telling an employer that you have not just decided to work in the field because you heard he had a job vacancy. Instead, they say that your interest and involvement in the field go back a number of years.

REVIEW YOUR STRENGTHS

A strength is any area in which you have specialized or excelled: top grades, extracurricular achievements, honors, or some form of recognition. Review your strengths and be clear about them so you can emphasize them in your résumé and interviews whenever it is appropriate to do so.

IDENTIFY YOUR WEAKNESSES

A weakness is anything that suggests you were a poor, irresponsible, or erratic student. Jumping from school to school, particularly from good to poor ones, failing, being expelled, spending successive periods out of school (one is O.K.), dropping out before earning your degree, and even changing majors too many times, all suggest academic and character defects which throw doubt on your ability to do a good job at work.

So, to begin with, locate all these weaknesses and star them on your list so you will be aware of the sorts of things you will have to avoid mentioning or even actually conceal.

TARGET YOUR EDUCATION TO THE EMPLOYER'S DREAM

Now that you have a sense of your strengths, weaknesses, and apparent directions, it is time to consider targeting your education. The first thing you target to is the Employer's Dream. Since, as you already know, the Employer's Dream is a general statement of what almost all employers are and are not looking for, this is a very general kind of targeting. It consists of concealing all your general weaknesses and emphasizing your general strengths. Apparent directions, on the other hand, qualify you for particular types of jobs. Therefore, you do not target these to the Employer's Dream but directly to the specific jobs you are pursuing.

MINIMIZE YOUR WEAKNESSES

The best way to deal with any educational weakness is to not reveal it. If it doesn't come up, it won't be a problem. Simply being aware of what your weaknesses are will enable you to conceal them 90 percent of the time. However, there are cases where educational weaknesses will show, and they will have to be dealt with.

One common weakness is having dropped out of school before getting the degree you enrolled for. This is always a potentially embarrassing situation, suggesting, as it does, failure and instability. The natural answers, such as "I got tired of being in school" or "I decided it wasn't really for me," are disastrous. The proper excuse is one that has nothing to do with school: "My father became ill, and it was necessary for me to make a contribution to the household."

Other weaknesses would be flunking out, changing schools with suspicious frequency, spending periods out of school, and the like. Unless the employer actually asks to examine your transcripts, which almost none will do, the best way to deal with these deficiencies is to write your résumé so that they are not apparent. Don't list all the schools you went to, only the best ones. Don't list starting dates, only completion dates, so that it is not obvious that you took six years to graduate and spent two out of school. Don't say you were in a degree program if you didn't get the degree. Finally, if you are challenged on anything, find an excuse that has nothing to do with school.

MAXIMIZE YOUR STRENGTHS

Now that you have minimized the weaknesses in your educational background, begin maximizing your strengths. Academic honors, dean's list, graduation cum laude, awards, or working closely with someone famous are all worth calling attention to. Just look for any accomplishment which might impress a potential employer with your past successes and future potential. It might seem an obvious area to mention, but you would be surprised at how many new job applicants fail to note their past successes out of a false sense of humility.

Don't overlook your nonacademic accomplishments, either. Employers are frequently impressed by membership in a well-known sorority or fraternity, an office such as class president, or a varsity letter. Remember, not all employers are one-time A students. Despite their present positions of authority, many were, and still are, very ordinary people just concerned with making a living and having as good a time as possible. An appeal to this side of them can often be more effective than knocking them dead with your past brilliance, particularly if you have none.

Whenever possible, emphasize strengths that are in fields allied to the employment you are seeking or that show you excel in roles akin to the ones you will play on the job. This, again, can vary from ultra academic to the exact opposite. For instance, a job in journalism may expect you to have literary interests and school newspaper experience, but a job in sales would more likely call for someone who was fraternity president and perhaps a popular athlete.

LEARN PINPOINT TARGETING

Up to now we have been working on general educational targeting. This is a form of targeting toward the Employer's Dream, minimizing weaknesses and maximizing strengths.

Now we come to pinpoint targeting, targeting toward the specific demands of a job by presenting and, when necessary, modifying or synthesizing apparent directions.

In pinpoint targeting we look at our list of the sorts of activities and roles a job will call for, as well as the general description of the field the job is in. We then try to provide apparent directions which make it look as if we have been moving toward that sort of work throughout the course of our higher education, if not for most of our lives.

Some jobs, particularly those in professional, scientific, technical, or other specialized areas, demand an apparent direction which is a direct preparation, much as graduate and professional programs expect one to have taken prerequisites. Other jobs are much less specialized and have no prescribed course pattern. Rather, they call for a certain kind of person, and any of a number of broadly disparate backgrounds can fill the bill. Even here, however, there are many backgrounds which would not seem suitable. Advertising, for instance, requires a sociable person with high intelligence, verbal abilities, some creativity, and a commercial sense. Anyone from an English major to a business major might fit in, but on the other hand a math or philosophy major might be out of place.

The basic principle is this. If you are targeting a field which is specialized, you must show an apparent direction that prepares you specifically for the work in question. If you are targeting a field which requires only a certain type of person, however, your apparent directions should show you off as that type of person, not aim you toward the job. In other words, research laboratories are looking for science majors, but advertising agencies are not looking for advertising majors.

HOW TO MODIFY APPARENT DIRECTIONS

Apparent directions can be modified or synthesized. If you are looking for jobs in areas of long-term interests, your actual apparent direction will be appropriate or nearly so. All that it might need is a certain amount of redirection or sharpening—raising a minor to the status of a major or elevating one or two courses in a given area to the status of a minor.

For instance, let's say you are applying for a job teaching high school. They want a social science teacher, which you are. But it turns out that they are primarily interested in someone to teach applied psychology, with the goal of helping students understand themselves. Your background was in urban sociology. There are two things you can do. First, you can emphasize and exaggerate the psychology background you do have so that it seems to be a major or at least co-equal with the urban sociology. Second, you can reorder your total program, indicating that the jumble of sociology, anthropology, and psychology you took was actually a multidisciplinary approach to the problem of understanding oneself in a social context and that you are interested in creating an experimental course in the subject.

Creatively reworking your educational background like this can be amazingly effective in getting some types of jobs.

HOW TO SYNTHESIZE APPARENT DIRECTIONS

Many times, however, particularly when you are moving toward a new field, your background will be far from suited to the job you are interested in. In this case you will have to cook up an apparent direction with very few genuine ingredients. Even here, it is best to build on reality as much as possible.

Begin by looking for anything at all in your educational background that suggests interest and preparation for the job in question. If the job relates to any of your long-term interests, you will probably find more there than you expect. Jot down all these ingredients and put them in chronological order. Now imagine explaining to the interviewer how they prepare you for the job. This will give you a good sense of what is missing.

Next comes the part that is mostly plain fabrication. Some

aspect of your background must suit you for this job. It should say that you are interested in the work and have been actively moving toward it for a fair period of time.

Does this suggest that if you are interested in a job for which you have no apparent direction you should lie about your background?

That is up to you. Many factors are involved, including the industry in question, how competitive the job field is, what your general qualifications are, how well you interview, your own scruples, and how desperate you are for the job.

Without doubt, an appropriate apparent direction is invaluable in getting a job. However, it is not always indispensible. You might get the job you want anyway; it will just be more difficult. If you don't want to lie, you might begin now to develop an apparent direction toward a particular kind of job in the future. Further training, graduate work, or a transitional job are excellent avenues to explore. In cases where the job you are interested in really demands specialized abilities which you have not developed, further preparation is the only route to take. But surprisingly, even many specialized jobs don't really need much preparation, just aptitude. Although the employer might want people with prior training, everything is really learned on the job. In this case, the trick is to do or say whatever is needed to get hired and then work hard to pick things up once you are on the inside.

The real question to consider when targeting your apparent directions is this: When the interviewer asks you why you want to work in widgets, what makes you think you will be happy there, and why you expect to be good at it, *what do you say?* If you have a strong apparent direction to point to, as in "I've been interested in widgets for years. Why, when I was still in high school I . . . and then during my sophomore year in college I . . . ," you will have an excellent reply. However, it is not the only effective one.

TARGETING
YOUR
EXPERIENCE

9

History is a matter of interpretation, and your work experience is a matter of history. This insight is the key to successful targeting. Your job history is a rich fund of raw material out of which you can craft a variety of backgrounds for yourself, each one suited to a different position. All it takes is for you to work with it creatively.

First, take the time to review your job history. List all the jobs you have held, or work from the job list on your résumé, if you have one. Consider each job, think about what it actually consisted of, how it was described to you when you were hired for it, and how you conceive of it yourself. If you are honest, you will probably find that your descriptions, even the most candid ones you give yourself in the privacy of your bathtub or to your family at the dinner table, are at best partial, inaccurate, selective, and designed to make you look good. In fact, there are enormous differences between what you actually do at the office and what you tell the world and yourself.

Furthermore, you will realize that these differences are largely a matter of description, of naming and labeling. For instance, you may have had a job that consisted of training and routing all the book salesmen of a textbook firm, and that job might have been called advertising manager; or perhaps you were the interface person between your firm and its advertising agency, and that was called advertising manager; or you were in charge of selling advertising space for a magazine, and that too was called advertising manager.

Even within jobs of the same title and the same basic responsibilities, what one does differs widely. The man in charge of advertising for one firm may be a relatively straight forward intermediary between the company and the ad agency while in another firm he might set basic advertising policy, choose ads, and help generate campaign ideas.

The situation is further complicated by the fact that single jobs with single titles often encompass many different tasks. Thus, the assistant buyer for a retail store may be involved in keeping records, purchasing, problem solving on the floor, making executive decisions, and evaluating competing lines of merchandise.

Not surprisingly, however, many of the same tasks recur in totally different-sounding jobs in different companies. Thus someone who has successfully carried out a management-level job in one company might reasonably be expected to possess or easily master, many of the skills necessary on an equivalent job level in another company.

This means that if you have succeeded as an executive in one company, chances are you qualify to handle an equivalent job in a comparable company. Most things you will have to do—giving and taking orders, facilitating company policy, and decision making, as well as passing the buck, looking good, and empire building —will be familiar.

This discussion is to prepare you to stop considering your own job background as a fixed and limiting fact of life, qualifying you for only a few similar types of jobs and restricting you from new areas. Rather, it is a much richer and more varied fund of heterogeneous experiences than you realize. You have been hypnotized out of recognizing its richness because you pay too much attention to what your jobs have been called and not enough to what they were.

When you free yourself of these limiting and often highly inaccurate descriptions and learn to reinterpret and redescribe your experience in varied ways, you will be able to emphasize the aspects of your background which qualify you for almost any job you want. This, of course, is the essence of targeting your job experience.

YOUR BASIC STRATEGY

The basic strategy you will follow in targeting your job experience goes like this.

First, look at your description of the experience requirements of the job or jobs you are going after.

Then look at your own job background. If you have a résumé around, use that to help remind you of all the jobs you have held. If you don't have a résumé, make a list in chronological order. Include job titles and a list of every major task, responsibility, and accomplishment.

Then, faced with a given job or job type, ask yourself whether your background, in its untargeted form, fulfills the requirements. If it does, how well does it do so? Could it be better? If you were an employer, would this job background turn you on? If it does not fill the bill, why not? What is missing? How far off is it? What is needed to make it work?

Once you have thought about these questions and have a general sense of direction, it is time to get down to work. The work you have to do is to redescribe or TARGET every job in your history so that it functions to qualify you for the job you are now pursuing.

What this means, primarily, is that each previous job should be presented in a way that shows it to be as similar as possible to the job you are going after.

Start with your first job after graduation and work your way toward the last (most recent) one, redescribing each so that it functions to qualify you for the job in question.

Before you begin, however, there are a few basic techniques you must learn. These are retitling, subtitling, redescription, reordering of priorities, and selective deletion of tasks and jobs.

RETITLING

This is the simplest and boldest technique, but you can't always use it. It consists simply of taking a job that was called one thing and calling it something else which seems more impressive or more in line with the target job. The trick is not a new one, and businesses have been using it for years to solve all sorts of personnel problems. Janitors are called sanitation engineers, head salespeople are called floor managers, and a large company may have five to fifty upper-middle managers with the honorarium of vice-president-in-charge-of.

Consider whether the positions you have held might be profitably retitled. There are many ways to retitle jobs, and, being closer to the fields in question, you will know best how to do it. But here are some suggestions. Titles like executive secretary to John Smith (the sales manager), can be retitled Assistant to the Sales Manager, while an assistant to the Sales Manager can be retitled Assistant Sales Manager. The key is to get the secretary or assistant out of the title, and also the boss's name, for that suggests you did someone else's shitwork for him instead of having responsibilities of your own. Titles that are vague and cover a number of functions, like Assistant Personnel Director, could be sharpened to Assistant Personnel Director in Charge of Clerical and Support Personnel. This suggests that you, although an assistant in title, were, in fact, in charge of one particular aspect of the whole, rather than acting as a flunky in all aspects. If you are gutsy and think you can get away with it, you could try something like Director of Clerical Personnel.

Another approach would be to completely retitle yourself,

pointing out the aspect of your work which you want to emphasize. For instance, a teacher who was also the part-time adminis-
trator of a particular program, and who wanted to switch from
teaching to business, retitled herself Director of Head Start program and wrote a job description that said, "Administered Head
Start program, hired and trained both teaching and support personnel, worked with government granting agency. Also carried
reduced teaching load." This replaced the accurate but unimpressive "Taught third grade. Also did paperwork of Head Start program in return for one-quarter-time course reduction."

SUBTITLING

When retitling seems unnecessary or prudence rules it out, subtitling works beautifully. Here you give your real job title but annex
an explanatory subtitle which defines the aspect of the job you
wish to call attention to.

Changing Assistant Personnel Director to Assistant Personnel Director in Charge of Clerical and Support Personnel, as in
my previous example, is an instance of subtitling. This defines
what it is that you did as Assistant Personnel Director. Sometimes
subtitling can be effective simply by identifying your primary task.
Other times, you may want to highlight one task which was of
equal or lesser importance than the others and make it seem your
primary responsibility. For instance, a college vocational guidance
counselor who, as a small part of his job, set up an employment
service for graduates, and who wanted to move into the personnel
field, might list his job title as Vocational Guidance Counselor
and Director of Student Employment Center.

REDESCRIPTION

Subtitling naturally suggests the technique of redescription.
This technique, which may be used alone or in conjunction

with retitling or subtitling, changes the description of the job to emphasize what you wish.

This change is not in the job title but the subsequent job description, where there is less demand for economy of words, and where you stand less chance of being found out if you stretch something, and if challenged you can always argue the point.

Here, that same executive secretary to sales manager John Smith can point out that she was in charge of routing and scheduling a sales staff and was not just a slave to the telephone, typewriter, and coffee machine.

Redescription is a fine way to make the job you had sound more like the job you would like to have had, and to help you get the job you are after.

REORDERING OF PRIORITIES

A subtle form of redescription is reordering the presentation of your duties to suggest a different order of importance in your total job definition. For instance, this same executive secretary to the sales manager might have done the following things in the course of the day: Brought Mr. Smith his coffee the way he liked it, straightened out the magazines in his office, paid his personal bills, typed for three hours, filed for two hours, given additional work to the typing pool, worked out all the routing and scheduling assignments of the sales staff, taken dictation, fielded routing problems, and so on.

This description reveals how trivial most of her job was, probably for reasons that reflected not at all on her actual ability. A description which reorders the priorities to put the most important first gives a much better impression, particularly when it is reinforced with a little creative redescription. Consider: "Executive Secretary to Mr. Smith, the Sales Manager. Routed and scheduled all sales staff; dealt with problems encountered by sales staff while in field; managed office, including other clerical workers; handled confidential correspondence; some typing and record keeping; kept office straight, made coffee, and ordered lunch for boss."

Obviously this makes a far better impression, but the inclusion of such details as typing, filing, and making coffee still leaves it clear just how valued or not her time was. Which brings us to the next technique.

SELECTIVE DELETION OF TASKS

In the technique of selective deletion, a careful choice is made of which job tasks to include and which to delete, based on the impression one wants to make. The final effect is to suggest, without actually saying so, that the included tasks made up the entire job. The example of the executive secretary to the sales manager, while benefiting greatly from redescription and reordering of priorities, could be made far more effective with a little skillful deletion. Consider: "Executive Secretary to Sales Manager. Routed and scheduled all sales staff; dealt with problems encountered by sales staff while in field; managed office, including other clerical workers; handled confidential correspondence."

Now there is someone ready to move out of the secretarial class into a managerial position.

SELECTIVE DELETION OF JOBS

Sometimes you will want to use the selective deletion technique not only for creatively redescribing what a single job consisted of but for editing your total job history. If you have had a couple of jobs which either look really good or can be made to appear so by some judicious targeting, and one or two others which are signs of different directions or just hard times, simply omit the lemons completely. The best way to handle this in a résumé, by the way, is simply to give the starting date of each job and delete the termination dates. Most of the time people will just assume one job lasted to the beginning of the next one listed. If you don't show any blank spaces, you won't have to explain what you were doing in them. This invaluable technique enables you to take an uneven and multidirectional job history and make it appear like a succession of good jobs—making you seem the logical candidate for the job you are seeking now.

You have now learned a series of targeting techniques for your job experience: retitling, subtitling, redescription, reordering of priorities, and selective deletion of tasks and jobs. If all these techniques were used to their furthest extension, that executive secretary of sales manager Smith could come across sounding something like this:

"Sarah Brown. Assistant Sales Manager and Coordinator of Sales Force. Duties: Management of sales force, including scheduling, routing, general trouble shooter and problem solver, participation in most other activities of office sales management, office manager, supervisor of clerical personnel."

Farfetched? Maybe a little, but it gives you an idea of how much can be done. Use these techniques judiciously for yourself, and see how much better you look and how much easier it will be for you to qualify for the jobs you want on the basis of your experience.

TARGETING
YOUR SKILLS
AND ABILITIES
10

To begin with, if you do not have the skills and abilities to do a job and do it well, don't go after it. It's not for you. The one legitimate concern in targeting, is to use the techniques only to get a job you are both willing and able to do well. If the job requires skills and abilities you don't possess, you will do both your employer and yourself a great disservice by taking it. *So don't go after it!*

Does this mean that if you want a job for which you are underqualified, you must forget it? Not always. Another option is to get the necessary training or experience. Nobody is born able to do most things; all the experts and specialists in the world had to learn somehow. A little investigation will usually reveal the best route to competence in any field, be it commercial art, computer programming, selling, or public speaking. Furthermore, most specialized fields of wide commercial application are taught in commercial schools which usually offer evening programs. They often have employment services for their graduates, as well. Other kinds of specialized jobs must be apprenticed within an industry, and here it is a matter of finding the appropriate entry-level job and getting it.

A warning: Everyone had to learn whatever it is he now does, but not everyone can learn to do everything, at least not to the level of expertise necessary to function on a first-rate professional level. Really successful artists, copywriters, programmers, salesmen, and other specialists combine training and experience with high aptitude and, in some cases, a certain kind of personality as well. Giftedness has a lot to do with how easily and well people perform. There is nothing sadder than to see people of potential and good general ability self-consigned to mediocre careers and lives of anxiety and self-doubt because they have become enamored of careers for which they have limited potential.

On the other hand, many of us who would love to change careers don't let ourselves attempt it, fearing we don't have the aptitude, when we really do. Get the counseling and help of people who are experts. For some fields, like computer programming, mathematics, and the like, simple aptitude tests can be taken. Verbal aptitude tests are a good predictor for fields that require a high degree of verbal facility. Many good teachers and coaches in artistic fields will give you honest evaluations of your chances. Go to one who is associated with a college or university, or who is very successful, to avoid the possibility of being misled by someone who wants you for a pupil. The same caution holds for the free aptitude test offered by commercial schools of programming, illustrating, and so on. They want your tuition dollar, and their aptitude test is likely to be a means of hooking you, not of giving you honest feedback. It is always best to find a source that has nothing personal to gain.

So if you want entry into a field for which you are unqualified, get an unbiased, expert appraisal of your aptitudes and then investigate the routes by which people in that field have become qualified. One might work for you. More times than not, you will find a way to succeed, and the training period or apprenticeship can be interesting in itself and even reasonably remunerative.

WHY TARGET SKILLS AND ABILITIES?

If the purpose of targeting skills and abilities is not to convince the employer you can do what you cannot, then what is it? The answer, obviously, is to convince him that you can do what you really *can* do. And to convince him sufficiently to give you a competitive edge over other candidates for the job.

FOUR WAYS TO SELL YOURSELF

How does an employer, or anyone else, satisfy himself that you have the skills and abilities requisite for the job in question? First of all, you have claimed that you have them, which is simply a matter of self-representation. Sometimes an employer will begin by taking you at your word, reasoning that if you falsify your abilities, it will show up immediately. The second way he has of determining your qualifications is by looking at the training you have had, formally or on the job. A third way is by checking the jobs you have held and your concrete accomplishments. And the last way is by seeing actual evidence—samples of your work, demonstrations of how well you can do something, scores of tests he gives or of tests you have previously taken. The rest of this chapter will show you how to target and really sell your skills and abilities and, through them, yourself.

IF YOU CAN DO IT, SAY SO!

Don't be shy. The first, the most important, and sometimes the only way an employer knows what you can do, prior to observing whether you can produce on the job or not, is from what you tell him. So speak right out.

As always, you must first know what the target is before you can aim at it. Get out your description of the skills and abilities your employer is looking for. Decide whether you have a sufficient degree of what is needed to honestly handle the job. If you haven't got it, forget it or, if you are really interested in that kind of job, get more training. If you have enough ability, make up your mind that you do and proceed to let the employer hear about it. He wants to know, in no uncertain terms, that you can and will produce for him. This is why he is hiring you. If you don't believe you can do it, he certainly won't. Some employers may let you prove yourself to them, but no one will give you a chance to prove yourself to yourself.

Another word about belief in yourself. There are many unsuccessful people who are better at what they do than others who are highly successful. The difference is that the unsuccessful ones don't believe in themselves and so fail to sell themselves. They refuse to take on challenging projects and responsibilities. If you suspect that you fall into this category, now is the time to take some positive action. Probably one of the best things to do is to see a competent psychotherapist, not a Freudian but a counselor who will help you to get in touch with why you disbelieve in yourself and to correct your negative preconceptions of your own abilities. Failing that, just look at the evidence in your favor. Does a review of your accomplishments indicate someone of competence? If so, pretend you are the person who did the things you did, and let the world know about it. That is, play yourself as part of your P-Image. Do it whether you believe in yourself or not.

TELL WHERE YOU LEARNED IT

It is important to tell an employer where you developed your skills. Keep in mind here that some ways of learning are more impressive than others. If you learned to act from Stanislavsky, to manage from the Harvard School of Business, or to write advertising copy from Doyle, Dane, Bernbach, shout it out. On the other hand, if night school, correspondence courses, and the public library are your background, keep a low profile on them, at least until you are famous enough to write your memoirs.

Along with the impressiveness of your training, remember its appropriateness. Businesses are on different levels, even in what are ostensibly allied fields. Small-city radio and TV experience is not going to cut much ice in New York or L.A. Managing the housewares department of Lafayette's will not relate well to a small chic boutique in Southampton. A degree in chemistry from a small liberal arts college with a weak science department is not going to impress a high-powered research corporation, and it might not even get you into a good graduate school. So if your training is inappropriate, play it down and explore other ways of proving yourself.

Suppose you have gotten your training and experience at a relatively unimpressive school but have also spent some time at a more formidable institution. It might be that you really learned everything you know about Frammis vector analysis from this brilliant little professor who was misplaced at Okee Phenokee normal school and was later sent to the funny farm, and your MIT experience was total bullshit, but nobody need know that. Remember the professor in your prayers if you feel guilty, but attribute your genius to MIT. The principle should be obvious, but if it is not, let me lay it out: When targeting your abilities and skills, attribute as much as possible to the most prestigious and appropriate sources and as little as possible to the rest, no matter where you really learned what you know. Furthermore, if there are any real disasters in your background, try not to mention them at all, even at the risk of seeming slightly shy on experience.

TELL WHAT YOU'VE DONE AND WHERE

You told them what you can do, you told them where you learned to do it. Now tell them where you did it and what you accomplished there.

Here we are emphasizing accomplishment, not training. What you do is to single out any accomplishments in your background which document that you have the skills and abilities you actually possess, and then prove that you have used them to good effect in the past.

Just fulfilling a function on the job which used the skills and abilities you are claiming is an accomplishment in itself. Just how big an accomplishment it was depends on how big the job was.

Further accomplishments are things you can actually isolate and point to. Setting up a new department, writing a successful campaign, cutting costs or raising productivity, designing a building: whatever you have done, if it is appropriate, point to it.

Targeting here consists of two things: selecting the right accomplishments and creatively presenting them in the best light to win recognition for the skills and abilities that went into them. Selecting the right accomplishments is a relatively straightforward matter of examining everything you have done and seeing which achievements correspond to the requirements of the job under consideration. The targeting comes in when you see that your accomplishments are really not adequate. There are a number of things you can do to reinforce your application.

Upgrade a Job

In some jobs, you will have performed the sort of work which would document your claim to certain abilities. In targeting, you can make it sound like the desirable aspect of these jobs was the primary, even the only, thing you did there. You already worked with this principle in the last chapter.

Sometimes a job you have had will be appropriate and will document the fact that you have worked with the skills you are claiming to have. But you may not have had any real accomplishments to boast of there. Instead, you just moved along fulfilling your responsibilities and sustaining ongoing projects and commitments. In a case like this, the thing to do is to claim a little credit where credit is not due. Say that you started, initiated, changed, designed, increased the profitability of, or dreamed up something which was under way all the time but which no one else has obviously taken the credit for. Nobody will be the wiser or the poorer for it, and you may be the richer.

Other times, you will have had a minor role in some important accomplishment. When this happens, it may be possible to claim a larger part than you really played. If there is no one around to contradict you, you can take credit for the whole thing. You can try the "I really did all the creative work and my boss got all the credit" ploy.

Emphasize Recognition

The thing that really elevates an accomplishment into an outstanding recommendation is recognition. A raise, a promotion, an award, a prestigious contract, a mention in a professional journal, a trend set in the industry—anything you did, or can take some of the credit for, that got any kind of recognition will reinforce your claim to superlative skills and abilities and will get you the best jobs on your own terms, without fail. So if there is any way you can lay claim to some recognition, do so.

HOW TO LET THE EVIDENCE SPEAK FOR ITSELF

Finally, there are some abilities and skills that best speak for themselves, areas where no amount of training and background is as eloquent as a little evidence, a demonstration, a sample, or some other more or less concrete proof of accomplishment. If you offer skills and abilities that can be sold in this way, come prepared to show them in their best possible light.

Demonstrations

One of the simplest ways to prove you have a particular ability or skill is to demonstrate it. Many clerical and office skills—typing, steno, and business-machine operation—are best documented through a demonstration. Sometimes an employer will ask you to type a letter or to take dictation. An employment agency itself may test you and certify the results to the employer. All that needs to be said about this sort of demonstration is that you should have the skills you claim. It is best to practice the night before and warm up before the interview.

Tests

Occasionally, more complex skills and abilities are demonstrated in this way, but this is a fairly unusual and irregular occurrence. What will happen more often is that applicants for complex high-skill jobs will be asked to take some sort of test. The test is, in fact, a compressed and prestructured demonstration.

Executive-level tests in industry vary from the highly predictive tests given in fields like programming to dubious examinations of potential and character cooked up by the personnel directors of large corporations. Tests of the first kind are valid and often valuable. There is no sense in trying to beat them; all you would gain is to sneak your way into a field where your aptitude is weaker than it should be for success. On the other hand, tests of the second type tend to be of little value. If you want to work in a place that puts one of these tests in your way, there is every reason to try and beat it as best you can.

Unfortunately, how to go about this is a major topic in itself which could be the subject of another book. The key, however, to doing well on any test of attitudes and personality traits is to understand the assumptions underlying the test. You have to know what the test makers consider to be good and what they consider to be bad. If you know that, you will greatly increase your ability to second-guess them.

Unfortunately for you, modern tests are far from simple. First of all, the qualities that test makers are trying to find are not always immediately recognizable. Frequently, they are looking for the traits of people who are successful in the field, rather than traits which seem to be positive in themselves. Other times, they may be looking at patterns which seem to reveal one thing but actually suggest another to them. Furthermore, many modern tests have little traps built in to catch the person who is giving the answers he thinks people want to hear. Still, test makers are not as subtle as all that, and if you really want to beat a test badly enough, you can do it. However, it will take research and preparation. You need to learn about tests and test construction in general and about business tests specifically. All this information is readily available to the public. The best place to look is a business library or the library of a university which has a good graduate program in business.

Most of the time, however, this is just more trouble than it is worth. Unless you are seeking access to an industry where all the firms you are interested in put tests in your way and you are doing badly on them, simply do your best the first time around. If you don't make it then, move on to a place that is confident enough to evaluate you on more personal and realistic grounds.

Portfolios

Tests and demonstrations are a matter of showing the employer directly what you can do. A much richer approach, suitable to more complex kinds of skills and abilities, is to bring in documentation or actual samples. This is the portfolio approach.

There are two kinds of portfolios—those which contain actual samples and those which give indirect evidence of one's work, such as newspaper clippings, photographs, and the like.

The first kind is used mostly by artists and, to a lesser degree, by writers and others who can easily carry examples of what they do around with them. The second kind applies to a much wider selection of people: architects, performers, designers, and other creative people responsible for productions, institutions, and programs.

PORTFOLIOS OF SAMPLES. If you are an artist, a copywriter, an actor, or a model, portfolios are standard in your profession and you know all about them, or should. If you are just entering a field in which portfolios are standard, you will have two problems. You will not know the right way to arrange your portfolio, and you may not have much to put into it.

The first of these problems is a lot easier to solve than the second. However, something can be done about both of them. To begin with, portfolios in any given field are fairly standard. That is, the material is carried in a certain kind of case, presented in a certain kind of way, and is itself a certain obligatory kind of material. There is also an accepted degree of professionalism in the way portfolios are done. For instance, a model's portfolio can be just a series of photographs and a bio, but the photographs must be of the highest caliber. On the other hand, the portfolio of an art director should reflect professional skill in layout, creativity, unusual effect, and the interrelation of art and copy.

If you are entering a profession where portfolios are standard, get access to a number of successful portfolios and make sure yours conforms in the formal aspects of the folder, presentation, and content, as well as in the degree of professionalism and quality. It is often worth having professional help in putting together a portfolio, particularly if you experience any difficulty or doubt that you can do it well enough.

The second problem is what to put into your portfolio. If you are experienced, there are two considerations. What is your best work? What is the employer looking for?

In terms of best work, I suggest that you do not try to be the only judge. Attention to what others in the field respond to is important, since you are doing a portfolio to make an impression. Feature what others have shown themselves to be impressed by. This is not the occasion to confirm your faith in your own private inner vision.

When it comes to deciding what the employer is looking for, most of the targeting considerations already discussed apply here.

Feature samples that are as closely related as possible, both in content and style, to the kind of work you will be employed to do. If you have a lot that is suitable in this respect, you might do well to delete some other pieces. This is a way of indicating that you specialize in what the employer is looking for. On the other hand, if you are deficient here, you may have to show a variety of work in order to prove general competence and experience. It is best to slant your portfolio—putting the most relevant work first to give it greater importance and limiting other kinds of work. This way, the relevant work will not seem like just one of the many things you do, no more important than anything else. You may be proud of doing many things well, but your potential employer might feel that it is a sign you won't be satisfied working for him and will soon be moving on.

PORTFOLIOS OF INDIRECT EVIDENCE. Frequently, portfolios can be used to stunning advantage in areas where they are not routinely employed. If you are at all creative, ask yourself whether a portfolio can be used to dramatize your achievements to an employer. Descriptions, samples, artifacts, or evidence of any sort can be pulled together into a montage that can give you an enormous advantage in selling yourself. A client of mine had just returned from serving in the Peace Corps, which he had joined right after graduating from college. His résumé indicated that he had spent two years in rural areas of Peru, helping villagers set up irrigation systems and modernize farming practices.

This, unfortunately, had virtually no effect at all on the job interviewers, who had little idea of what went into this kind of work, were unimpressed by it, and didn't see its application to their business. Consequently, they passed over him in favor of candidates with business experience. The applicant then created a portfolio of his Peace Corps experience. It contained pictures of farm regions before and after the modern practices he instituted, as well as pictures of himself with villagers, in the company of the mayor, at the agricultural college. It also contained newspaper clippings in Spanish, with translations, from the local papers talking about what he had accomplished and the resultant controversy in the village over old and new ways of farming. Along with these photographs and clippings were some brief descriptions of what his training had consisted of, what problems he had encountered, and how he had solved them. The effect of this presentation was electric. He got several extremely attractive job offers.

If you decide to present your own background in portfolio form and you are having trouble doing it, don't hesitate to get help. Consult both a designer and a writer. However, be cautious. If you make your portfolio look like a professional production, it will seem suspicious in a field where professional portfolios themselves are not the norm. Rather, have it look like the work of a talented amateur.

At this point, you have seen all the basic ways of presenting your skills and abilities to convince the interviewer that you really possess them in good enough measure to do the job. Some of these techniques will be relevant to your particular situation, some will not. It is important that you decide what approaches to targeting your skills and abilities you will use, and then take the time to prepare them with the utmost care, skill, and creativity. Remember that in targeting, the process of self-examination and preparation is just as important as actually presenting yourself to the potential employer.

TARGETING
YOUR PERSONAL IMAGE,
OR
HOW PEOPLE
REALLY GET HIRED
11

This is what you have been wanting to know all along but have been afraid to ask: How do people really get hired?

Well, surprisingly enough, there is an answer to this question. It is an answer that very few people know. Yet it contains the key to really successful job getting.

THE FIVE STAGES IN HIRING

There are five essential stages to the process of getting hired, and unless the circumstances are extremely unusual, such as being the boss's son or the only applicant who can program COBOL while swimming underwater, you will have to qualify successfully at each stage to get the job.

DO YOU PASS THE PRESCREENING?

The first stage is Prescreening. This is what happens to your application before you get a chance to be interviewed seriously. In some places it is a matter of looking over your résumé or application. In others it includes a preliminary interview, a covert looking over by the person who receives your application. Or perhaps you will be subjected to a routine interview in the personnel department to make sure that your basic qualifications, both formal and personal, are sufficient so that someone higher up won't be totally wasting his time by interviewing you.

This prescreening stage is sometimes just a matter of presenting yourself or your qualifications well. A good résumé, an appropriate background, and the ability to dress and comport yourself properly are sufficient. However, in the case of highly competitive jobs, the prescreening may be extremely selective and only a small percentage of résumés will be responded to. This of course underscores the importance of a properly targeted résumé and cover letter.

Once you pass prescreening, you are up for at least preliminary consideration. You will be interviewed by the person who has the ability to recommend you for the job or, at least, to the person who will make the final decision. Some companies, of course, have more complicated structures, and you must be interviewed by members of a team or up a managerial hierarchy, but the basic principles remain the same.

The interviewer, whether he or someone else has prescreened you, usually assumes that by this time you are at least qualified enough to spend time talking to. So your basic qualifications will not be his immediate concern.

ARE YOU "OUR KIND OF PEOPLE"?

At this stage, what the interviewer will be asking himself, consciously or not, is simply whether you are the right kind of person. Do you fit in, do you feel right, will you belong, will people feel comfortable with you?

This is the second stage. If you don't pass, forget it; you've had it. The interviewer won't let himself have any further positive reactions to you, either as a person or as a professional. He is not going to want to hire you, and he is going to program himself to find fault with you for the rest of the interview.

If you have flunked this stage, and often you will know it right away, the best thing is to terminate the rest of the interview as quickly as is polite and to discount the rest of the interviewer's responses toward you, since they will be negatively biased. The one thing you can still get out of the interview, if you are interested, is a sense of that company, why they don't perceive you as their kind of person, and what you could do to change that impression with a similarly minded company, should you choose to.

DO THEY LIKE YOU?

The third stage, and this is one you won't get to unless you pass the second one, is being liked. But remember, the interviewer will not let himself like you unless he has perceived you as the right kind of person. This, by the way, has little to do with liking you in a more general personal sense. He might have no trouble liking you at the local watering hole or on the squash court. But if you are not the right kind of person, liking you at the interview would either compromise his judgment or face him with the conflict of rejecting someone he feels friendly toward. He simply cannot allow himself to do it.

Liking you, by the way, is a complicated business. It is not just a matter of appreciating your style. The interviewer must feel comfortable and safe with you and, finally, must have a feeling of wanting to be associated with you. We will talk more about liking shortly.

Once the interviewer likes you, he is in the emotional state of wanting to hire you. At this point you are most of the way home, and only an incompetent interviewing technique on your part, very bad luck, or really serious competition will get in your way.

DO THEY WANT WHAT YOU HAVE TO OFFER?

When you have gotten to this stage, the real focus of the interview will swing back to your qualifications. Now that the interviewer feels right about you and would like to hire you, he needs to feel that it would be a good business decision. Essentially, he needs a reason to hire you. That reason must come in the form of a perception of what you can offer to the job that you are being considered for.

This is the time to start using the targeting techniques we have talked about, as well as some of the interviewing techniques to come in the next section, and to show the employer an impressive and believable array of accomplishments that prove you will be a productive member of the organization.

If you successfully target your P-Image and self-presentation to his needs, he will become enthusiastic about you as a person who can contribute to his company. He will just about have made up his mind to hire you—unless someone much better comes along soon. But, of course, as soon as he comes to this decision, he will be beset by anxiety, self-doubt, and ambivalence, as everyone is who has to make decisions of this type.

HAVE THEY MADE THE RIGHT DECISION?

At this point, he will want to reassure himself that he has made the right decision, that you are a competent person with a proven record of accomplishment, and that other employers have found you a worthwhile employee. And so now he will take a close look at your total background. Perhaps he will even check some of your references, to assure himself that you are who you present yourself to be and that he is not being deceived in some way. He may also have some members of the company talk to you, to double check and, primarily, to share the burden of responsibility.

These, then are the five stages of getting a job: prescreening, being perceived as their kind of person, being liked, giving them adequate reason to hire you, and reassuring them that they have made the right decision. Pass them successfully, and you are in.

This book, as you probably realize by now, is directed at giving you the skills to pass through these five stages. However, two of them, being perceived as the right kind of person and being liked, have a lot to do with targeting your personal image, and so we will talk more about them in this chapter.

HOW TO FIT IN

What determines whether one is perceived as the right kind of person? A number of factors come into play here, and they vary in degree of importance. They also differ according to whether or not it is possible to simulate them.

The variation is considerable. Industries like Wall Street banking contain companies which are virtual clubs for the sons of old WASP families, and there is practically no way someone not from that background could infiltrate them. In many other industries, however, all that is asked by most companies is an acceptable standard of middle-class business dress, proper behavior, and a sharing of the basic attitudes and values endemic to the industry.

This chapter is geared toward the more open companies, since breaking into a company which is a club for people of a specific background requires far more of you than targeting your personal image; it requires you to be a skilled imposter. There is seldom need for that degree of deception, since there are ample career opportunities of all sorts which are not hampered by this extreme sort of discrimination.

PLAN YOUR APPEARANCE

One very important factor is your appearance. But appearance only works one way, to disqualify you. Proper appearance is taken for granted and will not get you hired. However, improper appearance will knock you out of the ballgame instantly. There is no hard and fast rule concerning appearance, since there are variations in different regions of the country, between rural and urban areas, and from industry to industry.

The best guideline, of course, is to dress "as they do." Furthermore, dress like the members of the company on your level of rank, not like the chairman of the board, who, if he likes, may arrive in golfing shorts and two-tone sunglasses with electric wipers. As a corollary to this, never try to distinguish yourself through your dress, except by its correctness and impeccability. If you must, you can distinguish yourself through one small, unusual accessory, like cufflinks for men or a scarf for women. But the rest must be absolutely correct, and the one accessory should be valuable or have an interesting story attached to it.

One caution to emphasize here: Do not invest your ego in an individualistic appearance. I have met several highly competent executives who insisted on dressing idiosyncratically. When questioned, they all had rationalizations like "I'm good enough to dress the way I want," or "I'm hired for what I do, not the way I dress," or "If they want me, they will accept me for myself." To their credit, these men were employed in responsible positions and doing fairly well. However, they were all in the regional divisions of companies that had their major offices in midtown Manhattan, and they had been passed over several times for lesser men. What is more, they tended to be doing nuts-and-bolts in-house management jobs, and although they held a good deal of responsibility, they did not meet the public, participate in higher-up decisions, work in teams with executives from other departments, or have the opportunity to climb the ladder to higher management. A simple revision of their appearances might have greatly changed all this.

This topic of dress has been well covered by John T. Molloy in two books, *Dress for Success* and *Woman's Dress for Success Book*. These summarize a considerable amount of research in this field and will give you much more extensive advice than can be done in a few pages here.

A few more words about appearance. Clothes and accessories are obviously important. But what people don't always realize is that all aspects of appearance are equally critical. For men, haircuts, manicures, and such options as whether or not to wear a cologne are important. In some areas a man must not be too well groomed or he will be viewed as effeminate. For women, hairstyles, scent, and the style of makeup are important. Frequently, a woman must very craftily find an image which is feminine and attractive to men yet sufficiently professional and tailored so that she will be taken seriously.

Proper appearance is an important task. Appreciate it, be prepared to work at it, and invest some real money in getting it right.

DEVELOP A PROFESSIONAL IDENTIFICATION

Unlike appearance, which can keep you from getting a job, other, more positive personal factors are effective in getting you hired. One of these is the professional identification factor. This relates to whether or not you are already perceived as being a member of the industry in which you are job hunting. If you are in or on the periphery of the industry, that will be a big help. If you are not, but it is an industry you wish to break into, learn as much about it as possible. Read everything you can find on it, books and, particularly, trade periodicals. Try to meet people in the industry, visit various companies, and talk to people about it. Learn the jargon and familiarize yourself with the kinds of concerns and problems which afflict the field. Then, when you get to the interview, you will be able to talk a little shop and drop some names. This will give you an aura of already being established in the industry and will vastly help you to be accepted as "our kind."

CAN YOU BE SOMEONE YOU ARE NOT?

There are, of course, many other factors, far more variable and more difficult to target, which affect the degree to which you will be perceived as the right kind of person. These are personal factors such as:

- Your background, in terms of family, class, education, and the like.
- Your cultural background, the way you speak, the things you are interested in, what you read, your preferences in entertainment.
- Your general life attitudes, *i.e.*, whether you are a male chauvinist or a liberated woman.
- Your politics.

The more you learn about the industry and the particular company you are interested in, the better your chance of targeting these factors. However, before you devote yourself to extensive personal targeting, there are some things you ought to think about.

First of all, many people have a strong aversion to trying to pass themselves off as something they are not. If you try presenting yourself as a Republican when you are a Socialist by conviction, or show an interest in football when you prefer ballet, you might find yourself becoming upset emotionally.

Furthermore, this sort of imposture is very difficult, and it is unlikely that you would put in enough effort to be successful at it just to get a job. There is a real exception to this. Sometimes people from a working-class background, having gone to college, want to move into the upper middle class because they feel a real attraction to upper-middle-class values and activities. Then, over a period of time, through education, the careful choice of friends, and continuing awareness of such things as dress and speech patterns, they might be successful in developing new class identifications. But this is not a process you can start now and complete in time to get an executive position next month.

Sometimes, however, it will be within your means to fit into a different job milieu with only superficial alterations in your appearance, choice of conversational topics, and the like, and this is often well worth doing. In fact, if you examine yourself in situations where getting something you want from people is dependent on their liking you, you will probably find that you already adapt yourself to their expectations to a certain degree. Now you might want to consider doing it more consciously and systematically, keeping a low profile while you make **observations** and then doing whatever you can to fit in better.

HOW TO BE LIKED

Getting yourself to be liked is critical. Being liked is a big deal in life, and if you are easily and well liked, you doubtless are aware of it. If you are not, it has been a source of difficulty which you have been concerned with before this. There is not much I can say to you in a few pages which is going to improve your prospects for being liked, if that has not been your lot in life up to now.

However, being liked in an interview is somewhat different from being liked in general, and there are some suggestions I can make. An interviewer is not your potential peer and should not be related to as if he is someone you have just met socially. There is a real difference in roles, authority, and power, and this requires a sort of subtle deference. That is, you let him decide on the basic subjects of conversation, on where you sit, on how long the interview will take, and on the level of formality. You always remain slightly more formal than the interviewer. It is his place to make jokes, put you at ease, and so on, not yours. However, you should endeavor to respond to any efforts of his in that direction.

On the other hand, the interviewer is not your father. He is a person in his own right, and he wants to be recognized, respected, and liked for himself, not just because he wields power.

So you want to relate to him in a warm and friendly way, but within the bounds of formality and appropriateness set by the interview situation.

If you are not a well-liked person, you should know that it is possible to do something about it, although it is not easy. There are a variety of group therapy situations—encounter, sensitivity training, gestalt groups, and the like—where you can get real feedback from others about how they experience you and you can understand what about you seems to turn others off. In these same groups, or in private therapy, you can then proceed to work with these aspects of your personality and change them. This, of course, is not something you would do simply to target a job. But if not being liked is a problem in your life, doing something about it could, in fact, change the further course of your life in a major way and make it easier, happier, and more productive.

Think about it.

In the next section of the book, you will find a much more extensive discussion of just how to relate to the interviewer. Make sure that you study it before you actually attempt any interviewing situations.

There are many more limitations operating on the interviewing situation than on a comparable social situation. For instance, in a social situation one might choose to talk about a great variety of things—sports, world affairs, the other sex, theater, you name it. In an interview, you might refer to some of these topics in passing, but you should avoid getting caught up in them. The appropriate business of the interview is to discuss things pertinent to the job and your qualifications for it. Other topics must be touched on sufficiently to suggest what sort of person you are, but not to such a degree as to deflect attention from the real purpose of the interview. The ideal goal is to give the interviewer an impressionistic overview of you as an intelligent, well-informed person, while pretty much sticking to business.

STAGE
FOUR:
PUTTING
YOURSELF
ACROSS

You have reached the crossroads in job targeting. Everything you have done up to now—re-evaluating your career, studying the Employer's Dream, researching jobs, and targeting your professional image—have been preparations. The next stage will take you out of your study and into the interviewer's office. Here your job will be to put across the P-Image you have developed, to sell yourself and get the job.

The following section will guide you in every aspect of this process: the art of résumé writing, how to use body language both to handle yourself effectively and to read the employer's true emotions, how to talk about yourself appropriately, how to recognize and elude the sorts of traps interviewers set, and finally how to close the interviews with a positive offer and how to negotiate for the top salary dollar.

What lies ahead is the most exciting part of the job-targeting process. But it can be no more successful than the preparatory work that has gone before it. So be sure not to rush ahead until you have built a sound foundation.

Good luck!

RÉSUMÉS THAT PUT YOUR POSITIVE SELF-IMAGE ON PAPER

12

As everyone already knows, if you want to get any kind of serious job nowadays, you have to have a résumé. Like the attaché case and the conservative suit, it has become a kind of badge of corporate acceptability. It is the first thing anyone requests when you ask them about employment, and if you don't have one they are likely to look at you as if you were unemployable. Aside from the fact that all employers expect résumés, however, nobody really seems to have much idea of what they are for or what should be put into them.

To begin with, let's set things straight by recognizing that a résumé has one purpose, and one purpose only: *to get you an interview.*

Another thing not all job applicants know is that the résumé, by itself, is incomplete. It is not meant to stand alone. It must be introduced by a cover letter. The cover letter has only one purpose also: *to get your résumé read.*

If you keep these two points firmly in mind, you will have a pretty good guide for composing your résumé and cover letter.

A COVER LETTER FOR EACH JOB, A
RÉSUMÉ FOR EACH JOB TYPE

Most people try to use one résumé for all the jobs they apply for. This works fairly well if your strategy is to try to get almost any more-or-less suitable job and if you send out large numbers of résumés, betting that at least a few will hit the mark. Targeting, however, is a far more precise process, designed to get you not any job but the job you want. In targeting, we make up separate résumés for each type of job we want to pursue. This means that if you are looking for three basic types of jobs, you have three different, carefully targeted résumés. In targeting, every application must count to give you at least a chance of being favorably received.

Still, there is a big difference between targeting a résumé to a job type and targeting to a particular job in a particular company. This is what we do with the cover letter.

The cover letter is written to a particular person, telling him that you want a given job in his company. The cover letter says, in essence, This is who I am, this is why I am applying to your company, and this is what I can do for you. Then it asks for an interview and says you will call in a few days.

The more you know about the job you are applying for, the better your cover letter can be. First of all, find out who the interviewer is: his name, his title, and his role in the company. Then write to him directly. Never write just to a title. Second, read the ad carefully and reflect the concerns of the ad in the cover letter. For example, if the ad calls for someone with heavy experience in selling advertising space, your letter should begin by stating that you are a specialist in selling space and that on your last job you opened up so-and-so new market and increased sales by 28 percent, or whatever.

Third, in your covering letter you should capitalize on anything else you have been able to discover about what the company wants, to convince them that you are the person to fill their needs.

The covering letter should be short, not more than one page single spaced and preferably less. It should be typed on a personal letterhead on good 8½-by-11 white bond paper.

Remember, companies are often bombarded by hundreds of résumés in response to their ads. Your goal is to get yours read.

Here is one example of a good cover letter.

438 West End Avenue
New York, NY 10024

Mr. George Ellsworth, Editor in Chief
E&L Publishers
575 Madison Avenue
New York, NY 10022

Dear Mr. Ellsworth:

I understand you have been looking for a new editor to expand your line of natural science books. This is an area of great interest to me, and I have some ideas that may be useful to you. One is a series with an ecological theme, organized around interesting ecosystems: "Our Shorelines," "Man and His Weather," "Food from the Sea," and so on. I have others.

My background uniquely prepares me for this sort of creative editing task. It includes oceanic field work (Woods Hole), teaching natural science (Boston University), editing (*Oceans*), and writing. I have just completed *Managing Our Oceans.* I am also active and well-known in the fields of oceanography and ecology and belong to several major organizations. It goes without saying that I have my finger on the pulse of both fields and am reasonably comfortable in most other branches of natural science as well.

I will call you in a few days to see if you are interested in getting together to discuss this further.

Sincerely,

Henry Silver
enc:résumé

WHAT GOES INTO A RÉSUMÉ

A résumé is a highly selective preview of your P-Image put down in a specific form on paper. Everything on your résumé will come from your P-Image. The opposite is not true, however; there will be a great deal in your P-Image that will not be touched on in your résumé. In fact, it is only in a series of in-depth interviews for a specific job that you will share much of your P-Image with one employer. Most of your P-Image will remain a resource to be drawn from as the need arises.

The résumé will call on all the basic categories of your P-Image: your educational background, your job background, your skills and abilities, and your personal image. However, you will primarily be emphasizing your job background and your skills and abilities. The only exception is if you are a very recent graduate with no job experience to speak of. In this case, you will put a lot of emphasis on your educational background.

For the average job applicant who has been out of school for a few years and whose work doesn't primarily rest on specialized professional education, the educational background will merely be a brief chronological summary.

THE THREE KINDS OF RÉSUMÉS

There are three kinds of résumés: reverse chronological, functional, and combination. The real difference lies in the way they present the meat of your résumé, your job background, accomplishments, and skills.

The reverse chronological résumé is the most conventional and simplest to prepare. In it you simply list each job, including the date, company, and title, in reverse chronological order. Each job is followed by anything from a few phrases to a short paragraph telling the reader what you did and what your main accomplishments were.

The functional résumé doesn't give a chronological history of your jobs at all. It just devotes a page to your jobs, accomplishments, and abilities, in glowing but nonspecific terms.

The combination résumé is essentially a functional résumé, followed by a very brief reverse chronological job history to document it.

All the other things that go into the résumé—fact-sheet information, educational background, personal data, and the like—remain the same no matter which form is used.

Putting Across Your Job Background

The employer is not primarily interested in your job background as history. He wants to know what you can do for him.

This means you must give him the following facts:

1. The job, its title, basic responsibilities, dates, etc.

2. What you accomplished at this job. Specifics such as increased sales, new program development, personal advancement, cutting costs, and so on.

3. What you have established that you can do for him, on the basis of what you did for other employers—*i.e.,* "I cut production costs 28 percent at Consolidated Clippings and can produce similar savings for you."

In a reverse chronological résumé, this information is included as part of the description of each job listed.

In the functional résumé, there should be a page at the beginning discussing what your responsibilities, accomplishments, and skills and abilities can do for him.

In the combined résumé, the functional page should be followed by a brief listing of the jobs you have held, in reverse chronological order and keyed to the accomplishments claimed in the functional part.

What Kind of Résumé Should I Use?

Both the reverse chronological and the combined forms are good. Perhaps the deciding factor should be the quality and relevance of your job experience to your needs. If your employment in the last few years gave you the kinds of accomplishments you need to get the job you are after, then the reverse chronological résumé would be a good choice. This kind of résumé conveys a greater sense of legitimacy than the others.

However, if you are trying to make a lateral jump from what you have been doing to something else, trying to cover up some deficiencies in your record or trying to establish the validity of some early experience over some later one, the combined form is for you. This form allows you much more freedom to target and makes it harder for the interviewer to pin you down. On the other hand, the purely functional résumé, the one with no chronological job history at all, should really be avoided unless you have no other choice. It makes a suspect impression, being all claim and no substance. If your job history is so weak, it might be better to send in no résumé at all, just a good introductory letter asking for an interview so that you can present yourself in person.

First Take Some Time to Review

Before going to work on your résumé, take some time off to review the targeting chapters in the preceding section. Look both at the chapters themselves and the actual targeting work you did along with them. All the principles you learned, particularly in chapter 9, Targeting Your Experience, hold here.

Also take a look at the first third of chapter 14, "Sit Down and Tell Me About Yourself." Read the sections headed: Emphasize What You Have Done; Use Facts, Not Adjectives; and Be Precise. These will be very helpful.

Then take out the job background you targeted for this job type. If you have not yet done this, go back to chapter 9, Targeting Your Experience, and do it now. This will be the basis of your résumé.

THE REVERSE CHRONOLOGICAL RÉSUMÉ

Start with the most recent job in your targeted background.

State the job title, company title, and dates of employment.

Then, starting with the most important and relevant, list the responsibilities the job entailed. Don't list more than the three or four main ones. Remember, in targeting it is not what was most important to you but what the employer is going to consider most applicable to his needs.

Then again, starting with those most relevant and impressive, list the major accomplishments you claim to have had at the job. Again, keep the list short. If there are a great many, you may list as many as six, but make sure each one packs a wallop. If you list trivial accomplishments along with significant ones, it will all seem trivial.

Now put the entire entry into résumé language, which is terse, precise, and functional. You should use the jargon and buzz words of the industry if you can, but only if you can use them well and if the résumé is going to someone who will understand them. Use them sparingly, regardless.

Either write in the first person, as in "I prepared all minutes at board meetings," or delete the article entirely: "Prepared all minutes at board meetings." Don't use the third person, i.e., "He prepared. . . ." It sounds like an obituary.

For the reverse chronological résumé, the deleted article is preferable. It is more concise and telegraphic. But for the combination résumé, the first person is better because it is a more personal form.

Follow this procedure with every major job in your targeted background.

Now go over the résumé. See if there is anything you left out or any way you can shorten it without omitting anything essential.

Do this again . . . and again . . . until the whole thing is precise, telegraphic, and extremely concise.

Do not try to do a résumé without a targeted job background. Your résumé is based on your P-Image. This chapter is part of a total concept and is not meant to be used as a guide to résumé writing independent of the rest of the book.

Here is a sample of a reverse chronological résumé:

Henry Silver
438 West End Avenue
New York, NY 10024

Work Experience	
1975-present	Wrote book *Managing Our Oceans*, to be released in spring by Simon and Schuster. Preliminary notices are good to excellent.
1972–1975	Assistant Editor. *Oceans Magazine*. Developed themes for whole issues. Conceived articles, then contacted researchers who were qualified to write them. In many cases, was unrecognized ghost writer for researchers.
	Wrote regular column "Managing Our Oceans" which became basis for book.
1970–1972	Instructor of Environmental Studies, Boston University.
	Taught on graduate and undergraduate levels. Began a student participatory program of Pollution Watch, monitoring waters in Boston Harbor, which is still operating.
1968–1970	Research Associate. Woods Hole Marine Biological Laboratories.
	Participated in all phases of study of declining cod fisheries off St. George's

Bank, including both field work (shipboard) and laboratory work.

Results implicated overfishing and got me involved in fields of ecology and conservation.

Education   B.A. 1966, University of Hawaii. Major, East-West Studies. Minor, Oceanography.

M.A., Miami U. Oceanography. Additional graduate work in areas directly relevant to projects I have been working on.

Personal   Married, two children. Able to do limited travel.

Professional Publications   *Oceanography and the Declining Cod Catch,* Journal Marine Sciences, Vol. 12, 1970.

Affiliations   Association of Ecological Activists (secretary); Association for Oceanographic Studies; Marine Biological Association

THE FUNCTIONAL RÉSUMÉ

If you must use a functional résumé, here is a sample based on the same person's background.

Henry Silver
438 West End Avenue
New York, NY 10024

SCIENCE EDITOR   Responsible for developing themes for entire issues, *Oceans Magazine.* Thought up ideas for articles, then got scientists to write them. Often ghost wrote articles. Did all standard tasks of editing from reading unsolicited contributions to putting magazine to bed. Edited research reports while at Woods Hole. Specialized at putting technical reports into more readable form.

WRITER

Wrote nonfiction book *Managing Our Oceans* to be published this spring by Simon and Schuster. Advance reviews have been good to excellent. The book covers the effects of pollution, fishing, and other human interferences in the world's oceans and proposes a new plan for global management as multiple-usage resources.

TEACHER

Undergraduate and graduate teaching at Boston University in Environmental Studies. Developed two new courses, the Oceanic Foods Chain and Living with Nature. Started the Pollution Watch project in Boston Harbor to monitor water pollution—still operating.

RESEARCHER

Trained in multiple phases of oceanic research. Participated in Study of Cod Fisheries with Woods Hole Marine Biological Laboratories. Both shipboard and laboratory work. Instrumental in rejecting current change hypothesis and implicating overfishing.

ECOLOGIST

Passionately involved in all aspects of ecology and conservation. Believe that man can share the planet successfully with all other forms of life through responsible planning. Specialize in marine ecology and, particularly, in public education through the written word.

EDUCATION	B.A. 1966, University of Hawaii. Major, East-West Studies. Minor, Oceanography. M.A., Miami U. Oceanography. Additional graduate work in areas directly relevant to projects I have been working on.
PERSONAL	Married, two children. Able to do limited travel.
PROFESSIONAL PUBLICATIONS	*Oceanography and the Declining Cod Catch,* Journal Marine Sciences, Vol. 12, 1970.
AFFILIATIONS	Association of Ecological Activists (secretary); Association for Oceanographic Studies; Marine Biological Association

THE COMBINATION RÉSUMÉ

To prepare a combination résumé, begin by going over your targeted background. On a separate piece of paper make the following lists:

All the major types of things you have been responsible for within the basic job category—for instance, new product development, pitching advertisers for accounts, account executive, campaign concepts, etc.

Then under each of these headings list all your major accomplishments in that area, taken from all the jobs you have held.

Now put the major things you do in the order that is most likely to be relevant and impressive to the prospective employer.

Do the same thing with the specific accomplishments under the larger headings.

Review the big headings and edit out anything that does not seem, on second thought, both impressive and necessary. You should end up with no more than six or seven categories.

Also edit the specific accomplishments. You should have no more than two or three accomplishments for each category, unless they are really so impressive they can't be left out.

Remember, whether it is the combination or the reverse chronological form you are using, the entire job background section should fit on a page, or a page and a half at the most, unless you have a very long and impressive background. And your entire résumé should ideally fit on two pages.

Now once again put the whole thing in résumé language, terse, precise, and functional. Use either the first person or, if you prefer, the deleted article.

After listing all your responsibilities and accomplishments, make a simple list of your jobs in reverse chronological order: date, title, company—no more.

One more thing. It adds legitimacy to this type of résumé if, when you mention an accomplishment, you name the company where you did it. Such as, "While at Acme, I set a new record for selling iceboxes to Eskimos."

However, if your résumé is heavily distorted, a little confusion might be more to your advantage than the appearance of legitimacy, so you might not want to do this.

Your Educational Background

Once again, work from the educational background you have already targeted for this type of job when you were working with chapter 8, Targeting Your Education. List schools in reverse chronological order, giving dates, schools, degrees, relevant major or courses, honors, etc. Just a simple list will be sufficient, unless you are a recent graduate. If you are a recent graduate, expand the education section in such a way as to make it resemble the job background section. Your educational targeting work will be your guide in this.

Once again, if you are a recent graduate and have not done the targeting work in chapter 8, you are not prepared to do an extensive educational background.

Go back and do it first.

Other Things to Include

• Your age, if it is in your favor.

• Your marital status and number of dependants, if that is in your favor. (This depends on whether you are a woman or a man, your age, and the bias of the firm. Refer to The Employer's Dream and chapter 17, Women in a Man's World.)

• Whether you are free to travel or relocate.

• Any non–work-related accomplishments which are impressive or portray you as the right kind of person for the job.

• Any other personal details which suggest that you are right for the job. For instance, insurance companies want to hire salesmen who have numerous club memberships and other social affiliations.

• Any memberships in professional organizations or prestige societies, putting first those in which you have held office.

Things to Leave Out and Other Assorted Don'ts

• If you want to begin your résumé with a statement of job objective, don't list more than one. Actually, you can leave out job objective altogether. It only limits your résumé unnecessarily. That is what your cover letter is for.

• Don't include a photograph of yourself.

• Don't lock yourself in by stating a salary range. Under salary, put "negotiable."

• Don't list former salaries.

• Don't give references. Simply state that they are available upon request. Whenever you do give someone as a reference, check with them to make sure they will be enthusiastic about you. A good trick is to ask them if you can write the letter. If they say yes, they are pretty much locked into corroborating what you say. Also, remember that nobody knows who your actual superior was on a previous job. You can give your best buddy if he has an appropriate job title.

• Don't give reasons for leaving your last job.

• Don't volunteer anything negative. If you didn't finish college or got fired from your last job, let them find it out without your help.

A Few More Do's

• Ask a few colleagues to look over your résumé. In particular, ask them to look for things they could take the wrong way. Incorporate their feedback if the things they say make sense.

• Put your résumé away for a few days. Then take it out, look it over, and redo it.

• Do it again.

• Do your own résumé. Résumé services are not expert in targeting; they don't know you as well as you do, and they don't care. If you have to use a résumé service, do your own targeted résumé first, and then give it to a service to polish up.

• Type your résumé in a conventional typeface, using an electric typewriter, on standard 8 1/2 by 11 paper and then offset on a quality white bond. No fancy typefaces, colored, odd-sized, or bordered stocks, or extra heavy papers. A résumé is a business document, not show business. If you use a résumé service, don't let them talk you into any of the foregoing gimmicks. Your résumé should look like any other impeccably prepared résumé. But it should read better.

• Keep your résumé to two pages—three, if you have been around a long time and have a tremendous number of illustrious accomplishments to your credit. Frank Lloyd Wright, on one famous occasion, simply wrote "consult your encyclopedia."

• Get a good résumé guide like the kind Arco Publishing puts out. They contain hundreds of examples and will give you ideas for how to handle your particular situation. However, be selective and do not do anything which violates the guidelines set forth in this chapter or that goes against the principles of targeting.

PUTTING
YOURSELF ACROSS
THROUGH
BODY LANGUAGE
13

Even when you are silent, you are communicating something through your body language. The way you sit, stand, walk, or fidget, the expression on your face, the degree of tension or relaxation of your muscles, all these things reveal your emotions, and sometimes even your thoughts, to others. On the other hand, you are always reading the body language of other people. Sometimes you do so unconsciously, sometimes consciously. Even when you are unaware of it, your impressions of the other person are affected by your feelings about them. This shows through your own body language, which in turn is being picked up by the other person.

Thus, we actually carry on body-language conversations within our verbal conversations. These "silent" conversations have profound effects on what is communicated in the course of an interpersonal interaction. And frequently they completely alter its course. Since most of us are inadequately aware of body language, both in the ways in which we transmit it and the ways in which we read and respond to it, we fail to understand and control these silent conversations as well as we can. Understanding and being able to control body language, then, is a powerful tool in manipulating all interpersonal interactions.

In the job interview situation, awareness and understanding of body language will be invaluable in two ways. The first is in being able to control the impression of yourself that you are projecting to the interviewer, and the second is in understanding how the interviewer is responding to you so that you may guide your presentation and manipulate him to best advantage.

PRESENTING YOURSELF

Unless you are a skilled actor, it is unrealistic to try to convey a great variety of nuances and impressions through the use of body language. What you should really be concerned with is learning how to handle yourself in the interview situation, controlling your body language to appear self-confident, assertive, enthusiastic, and honest without revealing or suggesting any personal weaknesses.

To help you achieve this, let's go through the entire interviewing situation from the moment you arrive at the secretary's desk to your departure from the interviewer's office. Here are some simple, basic ways of handling yourself throughout, including the proper way to sit, use your hands, and enter and leave a room. If you follow this guide, your task will be greatly simplified, and you will be able to concentrate on your verbal presentation without fear that your body language will betray you.

THE SECRETARY'S DESK

Consider your interview to begin when you enter the outer office and are seen by the secretary or receptionist. Sometimes, even most of the time, this will have no bearing whatsoever on your evaluation, but executives do tend to rely on their secretaries and consult them for an opinion.

When you enter, you will encounter one of three situations:

a public area with clerical workers behind it, separated by a counter; a large room with public and private areas, separated by space and perhaps different decorative treatments, such as floor covering; or a public area with a secretary/receptionist's desk in it or adjacent to it.

Go to the part of the public area closest to the receptionist. Do not pass into the work area. For instance, if there is a counter or a window, go to it. If the room is large with decorative demarcations, go to the edge of the rug or whatever marks the boundary between public and private space. If there is a public area with a desk in it, go right up to the front of the desk. Don't go around to the sides or back of it. The principle here is simple: Respect the demarcation between private and public space and approach the appropriate point where the two spaces interface, but never invade the private work space of the office.

Stand there fully dressed, except for your hat (if you are a man), until someone makes eye contact with you or addresses you. Then simply say, "I am so-and-so. I have an eleven o'clock appointment with so-and-so." Wait. You will probably be told where to sit and what to do with your coat. If you are not, use your judgment if the facilities are obvious; ask, if they are not.

If nobody sees or responds to you in the first two or three minutes after your arrival, you may call for someone's attention with a polite "Excuse me" or "Hello." Do not, however, show impatience or irritability, no matter what.

Now take off your coat and hang it up or fold it neatly and put it beside you. Sit straight, leaning back in your seat, but don't sprawl or slouch. Your feet may be flat on the floor or crossed. Your hands should be on your knees, in your lap, or holding something. Pick up and read the most serious newspaper in your region, the most serious magazine in the office, or if there is literature about the company or a trade publication, read that. Don't make eye contact or conversation with the receptionist. In fact, just to be on the safe side, don't do anything at all that anyone could possibly have an opinion of. Just sit there and read.

Soon it will be time for the interview. Either you will be given directions to the interviewer's office, the receptionist will show you the way, or the interviewer will come out to meet you.

Have your things ready to go. Your attaché case closed, your newspaper folded, and your coat, if you are going to take it, neatly and compactly folded. Nothing is more discomforting than having to hurriedly get your things together when someone is waiting for you.

Thank the receptionist. Just say, "Thank you," nothing fancy.

CROSSING THE INTERVIEWER'S THRESHOLD

If you arrive at the interviewer's office unescorted, what you do depends on whether his door is open or closed. If it is closed, knock, then wait for an answer. Then open the door and, unless instructed otherwise, walk to the center of the room and introduce yourself.

If the door is open, stand at the opening and say hello. Don't knock and don't say "knock-knock" or anything else cute. Wait until he makes eye contact, and introduce yourself. If he invites you in before you can introduce yourself, walk to the center of the room or directly up to him if he is offering his hand. Then introduce yourself, shaking hands at the same time.

Your handshake should consist of two shakes with firm but not excessive pressure.

SITTING DOWN

If he tells you to just sit anywhere, take the seat closest to him but not to the side or rear of his desk or private space. If you have brought things in with you, put them down neatly beside you on the couch or on a table, not on the floor or on his desk or any work space.

Your Posture Counts

Basically there are three acceptable sitting postures you can use. Each has different effects, and one must be used with caution.

THE LINCOLNESQUE POSTURE. This is the basic open posture. Your back is straight, either free or supported by the chair back. (By the way, if you have a choice of something firm or something soft and reclining to sit on, always take the firm one. It makes proper sitting much easier and creates a much better impression.) Keep your head erect. Put your hands either on your knees or in your lap. Rest your feet flat on the floor. Later, as the interview becomes more relaxed, you may cross your legs, but in the beginning keep them on the floor.

THE FORWARD POSTURE. In this posture you lean slightly forward toward the interviewer and increase your eye contact with him. This posture indicates increased attention, enthusiasm, or interest. Your feet may be either flat on the floor or crossed; your hands should rest on your legs. You back should remain straight, not slumped forward. And your head will, of course, have to tilt slightly upward to look toward the interviewer. Do not rest your head or chin in your hands, with your elbow on your knees.

Use this posture when the interviewer is speaking and you want to convey increased interest in what he is telling you.

THE RELAXED POSTURE. In this posture you slide your buttocks a few inches forward in the chair and lean back. You still keep a relatively straight spine; however, it can be relaxed somewhat. Your head remains vertical. Your feet may be either flat on the floor or crossed. (Flat looks more evaluative and crossed more casual.) Your legs should not be splayed out.

Your arms should be in your lap, on your knees, or on the arms of the chair. Never cross them over your chest, which makes you look closed and defensive, or fold them behind your head, giving you a superior and insolent look.

The relaxed posture indicates you are at ease and receptive. You should not use it at the beginning of the interview, but only when things are beginning to warm up and the two of you are talking freely. Also, you should never use it when you are speaking, only when you are listening. To do so when you are speaking will make you seem disrespectful and superior. Also, don't use it when things of particular import are being said, only when it is appropriate to be relaxed. On the other hand, use it strategically to appear relaxed when you aren't, as, for instance, during a salary negotiation. You can also assume this posture to put the interviewer at ease.

To summarize, the Lincolnesque posture is basic. It is balanced and open, alert and dignified. What is more, it is neutral and unrevealing. Begin the interview with it, and return to it whenever you feel confused or unclear about what is happening. It will give you neutral ground from which to re-evaluate and take hold of the situation anew.

The forward posture indicates interest, enthusiasm, and intensity. It should be used when you are speaking emphatically or enthusiastically or listening intensely.

The relaxed posture shows you are at ease. Never use it when you speak, except for brief responses, lest it give the impression that you are acting superior. It is best to use it when the interviewer is discussing light matters, to indicate that you feel comfortable.

Practice these postures, so that you can use them easily and naturally.

Control Your Extremities

If you are striving to give a positive impression of confidence, competence, and enthusiasm, despite being ridden with anxiety and self-doubt, you have to be careful that your extremities don't betray you. Once again, since we don't have the skill to use our body movements the way an actor would, to create a specific impression, we must restrict ourselves to controlling them so they don't betray us or give a bad impression.

HANDS.   The best thing to do with your hands is to rest them in your lap, on your legs, or on the arms of your chair. The worst thing is to use them in a compulsive, uncontrolled manner, scratching, fussing with your hair, drumming your fingers, fidgeting, or toying with something. You also have to be careful not to reveal tension or other negative emotions by clenching fists, gripping the arms of the chair, rubbing your hands against one another, or other uncontrolled movements. If you have trouble keeping your hands still, find something innocuous to do with them such as cleaning glasses, handling your résumé, or, if the interviewer doesn't mind, leisurely preparing a pipe for a smoke or smoking a cigarette. If you smoke, be careful how you do it. The style in which you handle your cigarette can tell a story, too. Compulsively chain smoking and viciously crushing out a half-smoked cigarette can be very revealing.

ARMS.   Your arms should not be crossed or folded in front of you. As I have said, this gives the impression that you are closed or defensive. Neither should they point, elbows out, from either side of your head like a pair of wings with your hands clasped behind your neck. If your hands are resting in a relaxed manner before you, as they should be, your arms will be at your sides, and that is the only place they should be.

FEET.   Impeccably shod, they should rest quietly at the ends of your legs without shaking, tapping, or performing any other independent gyrations.

LEGS.   Either put both in front of you, feet flat on the ground, or cross one over the other—not spread out, splayed, propped up, crossed on the chair underneath you yoga-style, or any other variations your joints might be capable of.

Facial Expressions

When in doubt, either a good serious expression or a full smile that shows both upper and lower teeth and crinkles your eyes are the safest expressions. Again, unless you are a consummate actor, avoid experimenting with nuances of expression. There is little room in the interviewing situation for sardonic smiles, leers, expressions of astonishment or bemusement, hints of inner wisdom, or any other accents you may employ in your private life. In particular, avoid any asymmetrical expressions like winks and crooked smiles, and, of course, if you can, suppress any tics you might be prone to. (Also, while we are near the subject, if you are suffering from a cold or hay fever, take enough medication to suppress the symptoms, so that you are not snuffling and rubbing your nose during the interview.)

Eye Contact

Don't avoid it, and don't stare. Make eye contact about 30 to 50 percent of the time. Use eye contact intelligently, when the talk is about something important. Don't hold it too long, and break it if it seems to be making the interviewer uncomfortable.

WHEN TO TRUST YOURSELF AND BE NATURAL

At this point, you are probably thinking that with all these restrictions you will probably appear like a wooden dummy. Actually, this is not true. With a relaxed, centered, erect posture, composed limbs, and a face that is either smiling or serious, you will appear to be an unusually mature and refined person. However, if you wish, you don't have to restrict yourself this closely. There are

times when it is all right to relax and express yourself spontaneously through body language.

What are these times? When the feelings you have are good
ones—positive, confident, interested, and devoid of negatives—
your body language will spontaneously project them. At times like
these, you can trust yourself and let yourself go.

However, even here a caution should be introduced. If you
tend to become overexcited or overenthusiastic, if you have a loud
laugh or any other peculiarities that you know of, be careful to
control them, no matter how natural you let yourself be in other
ways.

One other thing. If you are confident of your ability to charm
the opposite sex through flirtatious behavior, and you are being
interviewed by someone who seems responsive, feel free to try it.
With this approach, you may have your own style of flirting which
contradicts many of the principles set forth here. If you know it
works, go ahead.

READING THE INTERVIEWER'S BODY

Have you ever squirmed your way through an interview thinking
how much easier it would be if only you could read the interviewer's mind? Well, you can, to a certain extent, through his or
her body language. True, body language won't tell you the precise
thoughts the interviewer is having, but you don't need that most
of the time anyway, since you are already in touch with what the
subject is. It will, however, tell you what you really want to know
—the interviewer's attitudes and feelings toward you and toward
the way the interview is going. With this information, you can
keep better track of how well you're doing so that you can pick
up on negative developments in time to reverse them and see
positive directions well enough to reinforce them.

Body language is a vast subject and very largely an unex-
plored one. Researchers have catalogued thousands of gestures,
expressions, movements, and body attitudes, and just as many

have gone unnoticed. Controversy exists about the extent to which these gestures are inborn or otherwise universal, and to what degree they are specifically cultural. Many of them seem to be idiosyncratic to certain cultures. For instance, some cultures indicate yes by shaking their heads up and down and others by shaking them sideways. Other gestures seem to be much more universal, such as covering your mouth when feeling secretive or turning your head away when you are being dishonest.

When gestures are universal it is because they are a natural expression of emotions by the body. They are not transmitted from culture to culture but seem to evolve more or less independently everywhere. For this reason, one tends to recognize their meaning spontaneously, without the need for special training.

As a beginning student of body language, you will have to pay attention to these natural expressions of the body. And you are going to concentrate on your general feeling of what these expressions appear to be saying, rather than on trying to memorize the meanings of hundreds of movements.

To prepare yourself for this, you need to understand the basic principles of spontaneous body language. And then you have to begin consciously to notice other people's body language and to develop your own awareness and sensitivity to what it means.

SOME PRINCIPLES OF BODY LANGUAGE

Parts and Whole

People's bodies tend to express what they are feeling as whole units. That is, every part of them, from their facial expression to the set of their spine to the way they use their hands, reveals their feelings and thoughts. This confluence of expressions is called a gesture cluster. When people feel conflict, for instance, it shows itself as an incongruous pattern in their gesture clusters: they may be trying to smile through a tense face, or be leaning toward you as if they are interested and open while their arms are folded across their chests protectively.

When people try to control the impression they are making through body language, they usually manage only to control some aspects of their gesture cluster, while others escape them. For instance, they sit in a relaxed position but have clenched fists, or they look into your eyes with an eager, interested expression while you talk but still keep casting glances at the clock. These incongruities in their gesture clusters reveal their hidden feelings, as well as the feelings they intend to communicate. Very likely, you will pick up the vibrations of these incongruities on an unconscious level, even if you are not consciously aware of them. However, unless you really learn how to analyze body language, this degree of awareness will only confuse you or give you a suspicion that something is wrong.

By bringing a greater degree of expertise to bear, you will be able to clearly understand the mixed or conflicting messages the interviewer is transmitting. This will greatly improve your ability to manipulate the interview to your own advantage.

Inclination

The inclination of the interviewer's sitting posture in relation to you is very revealing. Generally speaking, his leaning toward you shows he is interested, involved, intent, and in some positive form of relationship. Sitting erect shows he is composed and emotionally neutral. If he is leaning back, it shows he is more detached and, possibly, feeling superior. He may be evaluating you, or it can also just be a sign that he is relaxed and at ease.

Direction

Another clue to the interviewer's attitude is the direction his body is facing in. It should always be toward you. If it begins to face away, say toward the door, the clock, or someplace else, it is a sign that he has become emotionally detached from the interviewing situation and wants to be done with it. Unless you can turn this behavior around very quickly, you might best terminate the interview and leave. Keep in mind, however, that his detachment might not be a rejection of you. He might simply have something else to do.

Openness

The best way of telling whether the interviewer is open or closed to you is to observe the attitudes of his arms, hands, and legs.

The arms are the primary indicators. If they are crossed in front of the interviewer's body, they typically indicate a closed or defensive attitude. If they are open and relaxed or, even better yet, extended toward you, they indicate openness and a reaching out toward you.

The next best indicators of openness are the hands. If they are relaxed or extended toward you, that is a sign of openness. The interviewer is closed to you if his hands are clenched into fists or if they are grasping something. Hands are also frequently used to shield parts of the face, particularly the eyes or the mouth. This indicates secrecy, and it is likely to happen when the interviewer is trying to manipulate you or is lying.

The legs and feet can also show openness. If the feet are flat on the floor and the legs relaxed, slightly open, or extended toward you, it is a sign of openness. When they are held close to the body and pressed together, the interviewer is closed to you. One caution here: crossed legs are a customary comfortable position and do not necessarily indicate closedness.

Posture

A person's customary posture tells you a lot about him in general, but nothing about his response to you. So in order to properly evaluate this response, first note the general posture. Then you can look at any changes in relationship to you.

A healthy posture, which indicates a healthy, non-neurotic relationship to life—and, we hope, to you—is relaxedly erect, head and spine straight but flexible, shoulders down. Increasing rigidity reveals some sort of stressful response to you, perhaps a defensive response, which might well accompany the decision to reject you. Slight slumping signals anything from relaxation to fatigue. Marked slumping may show movement in the direction of indifference or rejection. If the energy goes out of your interviewer, chances are it has gone out of his reaction to you. Conversely, if his posture becomes more energetic, he is probably becoming more involved.

Rhythm

The rhythm of the interviewer's movements and speech is another indicator. If it is measured and smooth, it shows that he is in full control of himself and that he is performing, to a certain degree. If it becomes animated by positive emotions, he is having a positive response to you and is sufficiently relaxed to express it. When his body rhythm becomes extremely deliberate, it means that he is controlling himself. An agitated and tense rhythm is an expression of the way he is feeling. If the rhythm is slow and labored, he is becoming disinterested and perhaps bored.

Composedness

Another indicator of the quality of the interviewer's involvement is the total composedness of his body and limbs. If he is sitting in a composed way, it suggests that he is focused on the interview and is taking a respectful attitude toward it. On the other hand, he may be going in three different directions at once, one foot over the arm of a chair, arms dangling, his face toward you but his body turned away. You can assume this expresses a lack of unified concentration and that, at best, his attention is only partly on you.

Feeling the Pattern of His Body

During the interview, allow yourself to be sensitive to the pattern of the interviewer's body as a whole. Does it seem open or closed, relaxed or tense, composed or dispersed? This pattern is your primary indicator of his feelings. Be aware of it in a light way, trusting to your intuition rather than constantly asking yourself whether his arms are crossed or his spine is straight. Otherwise, you will become so preoccupied that you will not be able to hold up your end of the interview.

Should you, however, begin to feel that something is wrong, consciously check on the details. Run through all the basic indicators in your mind and check him out on each. Is he resting his head in his hand as if he is shielding his mouth? Are his hands clenching the arms of the chair? Are his arms crossed or open? Take everything into account and don't let yourself be fooled by what you want to believe. The most negative body message is as significant as the most positive one.

HOW TO USE BODY-LANGUAGE FEEDBACK

Reading body language gives you feedback on how the interviewer is responding to you. It is like seeing your poker opponent's hand. It doesn't tell you exactly what card to play, it just gives you more information, so that you can make more informed decisions.

Uniformly positive body language on the part of the interviewer tells you that everything is going well. Body language which grows in enthusiasm and interest tells you that you have moved into an area which the interviewer is particularly responsive to and that you should develop that area. Body language that becomes increasingly defensive, disinterested, bored, contemptuous, or secretive indicates that the interviewer is flowing into such emotions. It is a warning that the interview is taking a negative turn and you had better do something to correct things.

Whether the body language is taking a turn for the better or worse, you will want to figure out what crucial factor is changing the interviewer's response. Sometimes this will be obvious. But when there are several possibilities, you might have to do a little experimentation. The technique is simple. If you have a hunch, bring up the topic again, at the same time very closely observing the interviewer. If his body language continues to move in the direction you have already observed, you have hit on it. If, on the other hand, it reverses, that's not it. Quickly go on to your next hunch until you pin it down.

PRACTICE BEFORE AN INTERVIEW

Reading body language is easy and natural. Just the process of living with other people has already taught you a great deal about it—more, in fact, than you would believe. In fact, you might find, if you examine yourself, that you are actually relying on body language quite a bit to guide you in everyday life.

However, an interview is a stressful situation and one where you are constantly on the spot. In a situation like this, intuition tends to falter. For this reason it is important that you practice reading body language now, before you have an interview.

Practicing can be a delightful game which will enliven a boring party, business meeting, or bus ride. Just look at the people around you, observing as much as you can about them. Using both your intuition and the principles you learned in this chapter, see what you can tell about them.

When you can't figure out what a particular body gesture is saying, a good trick is to try doing it yourself and see how it feels. Not only do our feelings tend to influence our bodies, our bodies influence our feelings as well.

Another excellent form of training is to observe the body language of children. Not surprisingly, almost all adult body language has its roots here. And children, being much less self-conscious, are easier to read and more fun, too.

A few weeks of practice like this should hone your skills at reading body language to the point where you can easily, and almost instantaneously, follow the body language of an interviewer—or anyone else, for that matter—and turn that information to your own benefit. Now get started.

"SIT DOWN
AND TELL ME
ABOUT YOURSELF"
14

Perhaps the most terrifying words ever spoken to a job applicant are, "Sit down and tell me about yourself." This is the point where, even for the most seasoned job hunter, adrenaline floods the blood, hands get clammy and begin to sweat, the heart pounds, and an infinite distance seems to separate our heads from our feet, our minds from our memories.

If we could get in touch with our feelings at this moment and, even more, articulate them, we would be able to trace this anxiety to an all-pervasive uncertainty about what to say which, in turn, could be traced to a number of questions: What does he want to hear? How can I tell about my achievements without sounding boastful? Where should I begin? Am I talking too much?

These questions rush up in a great jumble, overwhelming us, giving us no chance to answer any of them, much less figure out what it is we want to say. This chapter will forestall your anxiety by showing you how to talk about yourself skillfully, effectively, and relaxedly.

The invitation to talk about yourself is an excellent opportunity, perhaps the best, to make a positive impression on the interviewer. Before you begin learning how to talk about yourself, however, you had better be clear on what it is you want to convey in the interview. Once again, let us get back to your P-Image.

Working with the first part of this book, you have already formulated, tested, and perfected your professional image. You have also used it as a guide in writing an effective résumé. Now it is time to present it. In the interviewing situation, you must act as if you *are* your P-Image. Everything you say about yourself should be a statement of your P-Image. Every new question you encounter should refer to your P-Image. The way you act will be an expression of your P-Image. You have put a lot of thought into formulating that P-Image, and now you must trust it in action.

As you will discover, one of the benefits of having worked out a P-Image in advance is that you are freed from constantly having to figure out what to say about yourself. This enables you to concentrate on talking about yourself well, relating to the interviewer, and manipulating the interviewing situation.

HOW TO TALK ABOUT YOURSELF WELL

It's okay to talk about yourself at the interview. That's what you're there for. Sometimes we hesitate to talk freely about ourselves for fear of seeming impolite or egotistical. These feelings might be appropriate in social situations, but at the job interview they are clearly out of place. There, your mission is to talk, so do so straightforwardly, at length, and without embarrassment or apology.

EMPHASIZE WHAT YOU HAVE DONE

Interviewers frequently ask for your background, and, of course, they need to know that you have the required education and experience. But no one ever got hired in a competitive situation simply because he or she had the proper qualifications. What really impresses employers and gets people hired are accomplishments. Talking about yourself is a real opportunity to breathe life into your background by calling attention to your accomplishments. So make this your first priority.

To convey your P-Image, then, present your accomplishments, not just a chronology of your degrees and jobs. Organize your narrative around these accomplishments, using only as much chronology as is necessary. After all, the rest is in your résumé.

AN EXERCISE IN REVIEWING YOUR ACCOMPLISHMENTS

Richard A. Payne, in his excellent manual, *How to Get a Better Job Quicker*, lists ten questions you should ask yourself in order to get in touch with your accomplishments. They provide an excellent way of reviewing each stage of your career and extracting from it that aspect of your activities which is most likely to impress an employer.

For the following exercise, ask yourself each one of these questions for each job you have held, and answer it as fully as possible, being factual and precise.

1. Did you help to increase sales?
2. Did you save your company money?
3. Did you institute a new system or procedure in your company?
4. Did you identify a problem in your company that had been overlooked?
5. Were you ever promoted?
6. Did you train anyone?
7. Did you suggest any new products or programs for your company that were put into effect?
8. Did you help to establish any new goals or objectives for the company?
9. Did you change, in any way, the nature of your job?
10. Did you have any important ideas which were not put into effect? (The fact that your ideas were not put into effect does

not mean that they were not good ideas.) If you present them and the reasons they were not put into effect to the interviewer, your basic creativity will still come across. However, it is probably best to first emphasize ideas which were used.

Unfortunately, Payne's questions are not adequate for all sorts of jobs. They fall particularly short for academic and creative positions, so I have added some questions to cover these situations.

The following questions point up accomplishments in academic jobs:

1. *What research have you done?*
2. *What publications do you have to your credit?*
3. *What is the extent of your community involvement?*
4. *What teaching innovations have you made?*
5. *What recognition or honors have you received?*
6. *How has your teaching been rated?*
7. *What are your professional affiliations, and what professional activities have you been involved in?*

For most creative jobs—art, advertising, journalism, etc.— you will have a portfolio to show. In addition, you might adapt the following questions to your situation:

1. *What difficult or important assignments have you fulfilled with notable success?*
2. *What recognition have you received in the industry?*
3. *What new approaches have you helped to develop?*
4. *In what ways did you make your company more successful (winning accounts, getting publicity, getting hot stories, etc.)?*

Some jobs have unique criteria for success. If these questions do not do justice to your job, think of some that would. Then answer them!

Once you have answered these questions, you will probably

find yourself with a wealth of positive achievements to document. Now your problem is to select those that are the most impressive and that promise to make the greatest contribution to filling the needs of the particular employer you are meeting.

USE FACTS, NOT ADJECTIVES

Use facts—simply tell your story in a factual, documentary manner. Don't use adjectives—avoid trying to convey a positive impression of yourself through descriptive or adjectival words and phrases such as "successful," "great," "a top-notch job," "the best salesman in the company," and so on. This does not mean you should expunge all adjectives from your conversation, such as the "hot" in "it's a hot day."

When you follow this principle, you will discover that facts do speak for themselves. They create a word picture which makes a complete impression, hard-hitting and direct. When you convey the facts of your P-Image, the interviewer will recognize their significance and will supply the laudatory adjectives in his own mind.

If, on the other hand, you try to characterize your achievements by using adjectives, you will encounter all sorts of difficulties. The problem comes from putting yourself in the awkward position of sounding as if you are complimenting yourself, saying that you did a good job or that you were the most effective manager. To avoid coming across like a braggart, you would be forced to downplay your achievements, which means, essentially, that you would have to give yourself less credit than you deserve. Another difficulty is that you might create resistance and doubt on the part of the interviewer. Not only will saying what a great job you did fail to convince the interviewer, it may make him frankly skeptical of you. Fortunately, all these pitfalls can be avoided by simply presenting yourself in a factual, documentary fashion.

The following examples should increase your appreciation of

the value of factual self-documentation over adjectival description.

ADJECTIVAL DESCRIPTION. "When I was working with Amalgamated, I did a terrific job on a number of very important projects. My superiors were very impressed and gave me a raise, a promotion, and an even more important assignment."

FACTUAL SELF-DOCUMENTATION. "When I was with Amalgamated working in the shipping department, I proposed a plan for reorganizing warehousing procedures. The plan called for dividing the warehouse into long-term, short-term, and transient storage areas. This resulted in a 40-percent gain in efficiency, as demonstrated by an independent time-study survey. It also resulted in a virtual end to delays in filling small orders. Soon after this I was offered the position of head of the shipping department in the Des Moines branch, with a $4,000 salary increase."

As you can see, the adjectival description is vague, unbelievable, and sounds like boasting. The factual description, on the other hand, is extremely impressive. The interviewer has no tendency to doubt the word of the applicant; on the contrary, he will probably become excited at the prospect of having the applicant work for him.

BE PRECISE

A very important part of talking about yourself well is precision. Precision in interviewing means detailed description, rather than vague or general description. It tends to go naturally with the documentary approach, just as vagueness tends to go hand in hand with adjectival self-description. If you are conscious of the need to be precise and work at it, it will greatly improve your interview style.

OVERLY GENERAL DESCRIPTION. "I was executive assistant to the dean and dealt primarily with matters related to public relations and fund raising."

PRECISE DESCRIPTION. "I was executive assistant to the dean, which meant I was in charge of the fund-raising office, reportable to the dean. During my tenure I moved the alumni newsletter to a magazine format, doubling its size and tripling its advertising revenues. I also managed to increase alumni attendance at alumni week, largely by filling that week with events which would be of interest to alumni and which were, at the same time, money raisers and created publicity for the school. For example, last year we had a film festival which was attended by 9,000 people, 3,500 of whom were alumni. In my four years there, alumni contributions went up 79 percent. And the total funds raised by my office were over twice what was raised in the four years immediately preceding my arrival."

There are, however, some considerations which limit the degree of precision that is appropriate.

1. You should avoid going into more detail than the interviewer is in a position to appreciate. This means avoiding technical detail that goes beyond the interviewer's expertise, and it also means avoiding things like personal or intracompany details that are essentially irrelevant.

2. You should strive for brevity. Don't become involved in long, complicated stories. What you really want is summary detail: just exactly what you did, and just exactly what effects it had, in a clear, salient, and succinct form.

3. You should present things on the level of detail at which they are most impressive. Sometimes the title and formal duties of a position sound a lot more impressive than what you actually got to do most of the time. If this is the case, too much precision will weaken the impression you want to make, not strengthen it. For instance, don't say something like, "I was director of marketing. What that actually means, of course, is that I spent my time

checking on the expense accounts of salesmen and making sure that orders got filled on time." Here it is more impressive to remain vague.

Or perhaps you held a position which, on the face of it, seems relatively insignificant, but which actually comprised some valuable high-level work. Even you yourself might tend to devalue what you did because of the relatively insignificant job title, but if you look at it in detail you will appreciate its value. Summer and after-school jobs frequently fall into this category. For instance, you might have been a student assistant in the chemistry department, but your duties actually included sophisticated procedures in areas of original research.

In cases like this, it is best to present the details of what you did in a precise way but to downplay or be vague about the job title. In fact, you can replace the job title with a job description. For instance, instead of saying that you were a student assistant in the chemistry department, say that you worked under Professor Fritz, helping to test new polymer synthesis techniques.

EXERCISES IN SELF-DOCUMENTATION

Now that you understand the basic principles of self-documentation, the following exercises will prepare you to apply them. When you are actually in the interviewing situation, you will have precious little time to think and a lot to think about, so advance preparation is the key to success. Because you already have your P-Image and a list of accomplishments, you are standing on solid ground. However, your P-Image is relatively extensive and very general in organization. What you need now is a short form that you can present to an employer in five to ten minutes.

So sit down and outline those accomplishments and personal traits that you feel will best sell you to an employer.

Exercise 1. Outline What You Intend to Say in Advance

Make an outline only. Don't write a speech and then try to memorize it. This will only make your presentation inflexible, and you will sound stilted.

Be brief. Don't outline more than you can present in five to ten minutes.

Divide your outline into two sections, one for your personal background and characteristics and the other for your job and educational background. The interviewer may or may not be interested in both, but in any case it makes things much clearer to organize them separately.

Decide on an organizing principle for each section and keep to it. Here are some basic organizing principles:

1. *Chronological approach.* Start at an appropriate point. College is best for the section on job and educational background. Some point in adolescence or early adulthood would suit the personal background section. Then sketch in your accomplishments up to the present. Show how the line of development has led naturally to the job you are applying for. This organization is best for jobs where formal qualifications are important, such as academic, professional, and civil service positions.

2. *Reverse chronological approach.* Start with the present and then move into your past background, showing how each item relates to the present. This is less complete and coherent than the chronological approach but gives the interviewer a more immediate sense of you. It is also shorter.

3. *How you got to where you are.* This resembles the reverse chronological approach in that you start by explaining how you happen to be qualified and interested in the job in question and then document your case by ranging through your background and bringing up relevant information without regard for strict chronology. This method is excellent if you have had a diverse career that needs a good bit of selective emphasis in order to focus your background on the desired job.

4. *Highlighting, or most-to-least impressive.* Present the highlights of your career. Start with the most impressive ones; then, as time permits, talk about other, less spectacular but still solid achievements to give your background a sense of depth. This is a good approach when you have a few impressive accomplishments and a short time in which to talk about yourself.

5. *Most-to-least important to you.* This works like most-to-least impressive, except that the data are selected according to what you feel is most important to you. This organization is better suited to interviewers who are more interested in placing you within a company than in hiring you. It is also a good scheme for college and professional school interviews, since it reveals your inner motivations and growth patterns.

You may, of course, find another organizing principle that suits you better than these. If you do, use it by all means, but first test it with the following exercise.

Exercise 2. Work with Your Practice Partner

Now that you have outlined what you want to say, say it to your practice partner. Your partner should do the following:

1. *Time you, making sure you are within ten minutes.*

2. *Give you feedback about the sort of impression you are making.*

3. *Respond to you in the ways an actual interviewer might, expressing interest and disinterest at various points, asking questions, and challenging you.*

4. *Scrutinize your speech, making sure that it adheres to the criteria of being factual (nonadjectival), precise, and brief, that it emphasizes accomplishments, and that it is coherently organized.*

Repeat this exercise a number of times until you are skilled and confident. After each round discuss it with your partner, then incorporate his feedback into the next round.

HOW TO CONVEY THAT AIR OF SUCCESS

When you go in for an interview, you are already representing that highly optimized version of yourself known as your P-Image. But over and above even the P-Image, there is one thing that every job candidate must project, and that is an air of being successful.

What are successful people like? Well, of course, they have many diverse qualities and are as different as you and I. But they also have certain characteristics in common: assertiveness, an assumption of their own competence, a quality of being at ease, respect for others and an expectation that they will be respected in turn, belief in themselves, and an enthusiasm and zest for their life and their work. Sure, there are successful people who don't enjoy these attributes, but they are probably highly motivated and have some area of unusual accomplishment to offer. There are also some successful people with many additional virtues, but if you just concentrate on the ones mentioned here and convey them to the interviewer, you will succeed admirably.

BE ASSERTIVE

Successful people tend to be assertive. What does this mean? It does not mean being aggressive, although they may be that too. Nor does it mean being overbearing, or even too outspoken. What it means, purely and simply, is that you say what is on your mind, that you make a *clear and firm statement* of your opinions, your feelings, and your needs, whenever it is appropriate in the situation to do so.

It is important, however, to keep this stipulation of appropriateness clearly in mind. On many occasions, during interviews and elsewhere, you will have things on your mind which you choose not to voice, not because of psychological barriers to expressing your feelings, but simply because common sense tells you that this is not the right time and place to express these feelings. Obviously, the interview situation is a very controlled one, and there will be many things which you will choose not to express. Don't be afraid that this will destroy the appearance of assertiveness which you are trying to convey. It will not. Assertiveness will be evident in your style of expressing yourself. That which you leave unsaid, nobody will hear to criticize.

The most important thing to remember is just to express yourself directly and unequivocally. "I would accept a salary in the mid-twenties." "I feel I can do justice to that assignment." "I would be interested in working with your company." "I understand how you feel, but that wouldn't meet my needs because . . ."

It is important that you don't undermine this impression of assertiveness by making excuses or apologizing for yourself during the interview. Once you decide to say something, say it and then let it stand. The time to decide what to say is before you say it, not afterward.

Worse than making excuses for the things you say, is apologizing for who you are. Your P-Image gives you a definite and positive version of yourself to project. Don't undermine its effectiveness by saying things like, "I hope you don't mind, but," or, "I just can't help being . . ."

SHOW YOU BELIEVE IN YOURSELF

Another mark of successful people is the belief they have in themselves. Be positive about what you have accomplished in your life, how successful and how valuable it was. Be equally positive about your future. Never denigrate or express doubt about yourself. The interviewer will have enough doubts without your reinforcing them.

People often think that if they put themselves down, others will recognize and proclaim their true value. With the exception of our mothers, this is always untrue. If you belittle your own achievements, others will take your opinion at face value, and end up valuing you even less than you seem to.

SHOW YOU LIKE YOUR WORK

Convey a sense of liking your work and of having gotten pleasure and satisfaction from your previous accomplishments. People who are in positions of authority usually identify strongly with their company and look upon employee cynicism with a jaundiced eye. If you seem cynical, critical, or dissatisfied, they won't be impressed with your critical acumen, they will simply consider you a bad risk. Paradoxically, this is equally true on more menial and lower-level jobs. Employers expect as much enthusiasm, loyalty, and company identification from clerical workers as they do from management executives.

BE ENTHUSIASTIC

Successful people are enthusiastic. It is both part of their rise to the top and a result of their success. Sometimes you will meet a successful person who is not enthusiastic. But I'll wager that if you look further, you will discover that in the early days, when he was just getting ahead, he showed plenty of enthusiasm. Now he's just holding on to the position he won earlier and consequently, has lost his zip.

Enthusiasm tells the employer more than just that you are on the track to success. It also tells him that your energy is flowing, that it is not constricted by conflict, guilt, anger, self-doubt, or other strong negative emotions. Furthermore, it promises that you will bring your energy to his firm to make money for him.

Once, when I was in college, I was looking for a summer job. It seemed you could only get hired by convincing the employer that you were not signing on just for the summer. This meant, in my case, saying that I had quit college. This put me in the position of applying for a number of jobs in which I was disinterested and to which I felt enormously superior. Of course, I had no enthusiasm for any of these jobs and, consequently, couldn't get hired. Things got worse. The weather was getting hotter, the jobs, more and more dismal, and I was becoming even more apathetic. At one point, I caught myself limply trying to convince an interviewer that I would enjoy being a company informer, that is, taking various jobs long enough to see who was goofing off and then ratting on them. Fortunately, I was unconvincing and escaped this opportunity.

Many years later, when I was teaching and planning to write a psychology textbook, I realized that a major publishing company was beginning to do with textbooks just what I was planning to do. I picked up the phone, full of natural enthusiasm, and talked to the psychology editor, telling him that I was interested in what they were doing and would like to free-lance for them. He flew me down, introduced me to his staff, asked me if I could be available on a consulting basis, and gave me some assignments. This led to a lively relationship. Several months later, he left to join a new company, and I was offered his job, which I gladly accepted.

The moral. If you cannot get up any enthusiasm for a job, don't apply for it. You probably won't get hired, and worse for you if you do. The solution to a lack of enthusiasm is to go back and take another look at the chapter What Is a Healthy Career? A long, hard look. Remember, you don't have to be a data processor, teacher, salesman, or whatever else you don't like doing. Even if you have to retrain or move to a lower-level job in a new field, consider that in a few years you will be doing something you like, at a higher level than you are on now; while if you don't make a change, you will still be doing the same thing and still wishing you weren't. Besides, as the great psychologist Alfred Adler was fond of saying, it is not the time that you save, but what you do with it that counts.

HOW TO STRIKE THE RIGHT NOTE

One of the trickiest parts of an interview is knowing how to relate to the interviewer as a person, being open without being familiar, respectful without seeming subservient, or assertive without being aggressive.

Of course, the way you relate to the interviewer, like the way you relate to anyone else, will flow from the interaction of your personality and his. However, relationships reflect not only our personalities but our motivating premises as well.

The following section discusses the correct premises on which to base an interviewing relationship. You will find that if you approach the interviewer from this basis, you will naturally strike the right note, and the interviewer will respond to you in a highly positive manner.

DEMONSTRATE ESSENTIAL EQUALITY

The fundamental premise underlying your relationship both with the interviewer and with the rest of humanity is that of essential equality.

What is essential equality? Basically it is the realization that, despite varying achievements, all human beings are equally valuable and important and have equal rights. On a more immediate level, it is the recognition that you are anyone's peer as a person, including, of course, employers and interviewers; that you are neither better nor worse than anyone else; and that you never owe or are owed the deference of an inferior being to a superior one.

The person who interviews you will usually outrank you professionally. Occasionally, it will be the other way around. Whatever the case, the nature of the interviewing situation will demand that you pay a certain deference to the interviewer. You are approaching his space, applying for a job in his company, and seeking to satisfy his requirements. It should be clear, however, that this is just formal deference. It is simply the protocol of the situation and in no way implies a dimension of inferiority-superiority. In fact, if your roles someday become reversed, the spirit in which you relate to the interviewer should require no alteration!

Many people feel inwardly inferior to others and, because of this, need to create situations in which they are psychologically on top. Interviewers, of course, are as subject to inferiority feelings as anyone else, and occasionally you will come up against an interviewer who exploits his position in order to gratify his personal needs. Someone like this will try to create a situation of personal superiority by intimidating you with the promise of a job. It is completely up to you if you wish to play this game or not. However, it is a degrading one, and before you submit to it I would strongly suggest that you weigh these considerations:

1. *Is this job that important? Keep in mind that if you allow yourself to be psychologically subordinated, it will very likely have a negative effect on your attitude toward the job if you get it.*

2. *Is the interviewer someone you will never see again at the company, or is he someone you might be working with? If he is someone you might work with closely, consider whether you want to remain in a subordinate role.*

3. *Is the interviewer an exception in that company, or does he exemplify the way people tend to relate to one another there? Of course, nothing is all black or all white, but institutions do seem to have "personalities," and nothing will lead you so surely into negative feelings and job failure as working in a place that is set up to make you feel bad.*

If, after due consideration, you decide that the circumstances seem to warrant abandoning the position of essential equality, then by all means let the interviewer feel that you accept his superiority. But keep in mind that this is only a manipulative maneuver on your part, something you are doing deliberately and consciously, which in no way reflects anything negative about you. Also, try to do it without resenting either him or yourself.

But if you decide to continue to relate to an interviewer like this from the position of essential equality, respect yourself and respect him. Let yourself feel that in every way you are as good as he is, and refuse to do anything or accept anything designed to make you feel any worse.

AVOID PROJECTING NEED OR DESPERATION

You have been rejected in your fifty-third job application. You have just sold your car. For six weeks, you have been subsisting on peanut butter and Twinkies. There is a "Dispossess" taped to the front door and your hysterical family behind it. Still, you must avoid seeming to come to the interview from a position of need or desperation. If that is what you do project, you may get sympathy, advice, information about job opportunities elsewhere, even a handout, but you won't get the job. Very few businesses, even those which give generously to charities, allow altruistic impulses to influence their business judgment. Employers are looking for winners, not losers, and the worse your luck has been, the less interested they will be in you.

So whatever your problems are, present yourself as a successful person with a number of options and emphasize that this is just one of the jobs you are considering. Also, make it clear that you are *not* strapped for money, you are *not* anxious about your future, you are *not* feeling demoralized or depressed, and you are *not* suffering from any of the other afflictions, practical or psychological, which invariably beset us when we are unwillingly unemployed or unsuccessfully employed for any period of time.

In order to maintain this impression, it may be necessary to recast some of your ill fortune in a positive light. Always avoid revealing to an interviewer that you were fired or that you have been unsuccessfully looking for a job for a long time.

Perhaps you are presently employed and either want to leave or feel that you might be forced to leave in the near future. In such a case, find your next job before you go. Use your lunch hours, take sick days, make up dentist appointments and funerals —just so you find time in which to job hunt while you are still employed. If you have just been fired, try to work out an arrangement with your employer that enables you to stay on while you relocate. If you are out of a job and have been for a while, think up a cover story to account for why you left your previous job and haven't yet taken another one. At all cost, avoid giving interviewers the idea that other employers have found you undesirable.

Unfortunately, feeling desperate sometimes shows despite all one's efforts to conceal it. It can be picked up by the astute observer in ways that are difficult to disguise. Furthermore, even if your desperation isn't recognized, feeling it can undermine your interviewing success by making you anxious, depressed, overeager, or otherwise less than yourself. Finally, feelings of desperation will disrupt your everyday life even more than they affect your job hunting, and this will show.

For all these reasons it is essential that you do not give in to desperation! This, of course, is easier said than done, but such feelings are within your control. It will help if you understand how this sense of overwhelming need developed in you in the first place. Feelings of desperation are the outcome of a belief system founded on convictions something like these.

1. *I have to get a job soon or else terrible calamities will befall me and my family.*
2. *I have to get a job soon or I will never be able to get one.*
3. *I have to get a job soon or else I am a failure and will never be able to respect myself or win the respect of others.*
4. *This interview is my last chance; I have to get the job; if I fail, I don't know what I'm going to do.*

If you examine these convictions carefully and without hysteria, you will see that they are largely unfounded. We live in a semiwelfare society, and although the system is far from perfect, literate people are in no real danger of starving or being without shelter. Aside from unemployment benefits and welfare, you can hold yourself over with temporary employments like bartending or taxi-driving. You can cut expenses and liquidate assets: an expensive car can be sold and a house with a high mortgage can be temporarily rented, shared, or sold outright, if things get really difficult.

On a realistic level, the failure to get any one particular job is no more significant than the failure to get any other job. There is no such thing as the last chance. In fact, if your luck has been bad for a while, it is time to do something about it, like working with this book. It won't help to become hysterical.

What is more, if you examine these desperate convictions of yours with a really critical eye, you will see something even more startling about them. You will discover that they are actually designed to make you feel desperate! They serve as a negative form of self-manipulation. Frequently, we dislike doing the things we feel we ought to do, and therefore we avoid them. However, the part of us which is most in touch with the consequences of this avoidance then becomes anxious and devises dire warnings to control our more "frivolous" impulses. In this way we bully ourselves into fulfilling our unwanted responsibilities. The trouble with this technique of self-manipulation is that we forget it is a technique, and we accept the things we tell ourselves as the horrible, unmitigated truth. When this happens, we give in to panic and desperation.

Exercise for Those Beginning to Feel Desperate

    1. List all your "reasons" for feeling desperate.
    2. Think about how each one makes you feel.

3. Consider each reason in the light of the preceding discussion. Is it really true, or is it a half-truth designed to motivate you —but which actually makes you feel hysterical and trapped?

4. As you discover that your reasons are not strictly valid, figure out the real truth of each one. Do you have other options? Are things really as dire as you have been telling yourself they are? Rethink each reason for feeling desperate, and develop a more balanced view of your situation. Now, believe it.

5. If you have trouble doing this exercise, or if things don't look any better upon reconsideration, redo it with a friend. Maybe he or she will be able to help you see some things that you are not quite ready to see yourself.

LOOK ON THE INTERVIEW AS A MUTUAL INVESTIGATION

Frequently, applicants approach interviews solely from the point of view of trying to get a job, without also interviewing the interviewer to see if the job suits them. If you tend to do this, you are doing yourself a disservice. You are subtly putting yourself down by implicitly stating that you have no real options or choices and have to take whatever you can get. To come from a position like this is very similar to coming from a position of desperation. It undermines your self-respect and lessens the interviewer's respect for you.

Therefore, if you haven't been using the interview to investigate the company, start doing so. You will get a lot out of it. What you learn will make it less likely for you to end up in an unsuitable position. And you will be telling your unconscious that you are a valuable person with real choices. This will give you a sense of strength and purpose which will convey itself to the interviewer.

RELATE TO THE INTERVIEWER AS A PERSON

People naturally relate to interviewers as company representatives, people to impress and get something out of, rather than as individuals in their own right. But interviewers are people, and unreasonable as it may seem under the circumstances, they tend to resent feeling used just as much as anybody else would. You will find that if you look upon the interviewer as a person and understand that interviewing is his job, not his identity, you will have a better chance of developing a sympathetic relationship with him.

On the other hand, keep in mind the reality of the situation, and do not relate in a way that is inappropriately familiar or personal. If you err in this direction, you will force the interviewer to withdraw—just to maintain an appropriate distance. So while it is important that you do not treat him just as a means to a job, you should not relate to him too informally either, as if the encounter were a social one.

LIKE THE INTERVIEWER

Face it, you are going to have a much better chance of getting hired if the interviewer likes you. And nothing is quite so effective in getting someone to like you as showing that you like him. The problem here is that if you merely fake it, trying to act as though you like the interviewer, you might well give an impression of insincerity. This is not the place for an acting lesson, nor should that be necessary. Rather, concentrate on the interviewer's likable aspects; most people have them. Then simply let yourself like him. If you can't find something to like in him, find something to admire or at least respect and let that positive emotion show.

THE INTERVIEW AS A CONVERSATION

An interview is like any other conversation. If you don't care which way it goes, you can just say whatever comes into your head and let whatever happens happen. But if you want it to go in any particular fashion, you have to direct it. This section contains pointers on how to manipulate the interview as a conversation so that it flows freely and satisfies not only the needs of the interviewer but your needs as well.

BE TALKATIVE

Sometimes when we are unsure of ourselves, our instinctive response is to say nothing. At other times we are reticent for fear of sounding immodest. Whatever the real or imagined virtues of silence, the interview is not the time for it. The interviewer is trying to draw you out. If you are reticent or laconic, you will make his job doubly difficult—he will have to work harder to draw you out, and he will have less information on which to base his decision. Both these factors will work against you. In fact, the only time reticence might work in your favor is when you are holding something back and can't think of a cover story. If you have developed your P-Image, this difficulty should never arise.

By making the interviewer's job easier, being talkative will pay dividends for you. He will take a more positive attitude toward your application, and he will get the impression that you are a person who is open and at ease.

STICK TO THE POINT

However, if you are going to be talkative, there are a few things you should keep in mind. The first is to stick to the point. The purpose of being talkative is to help the interviewer get the information he is after. So pay attention to his questions and answer fully without changing the subject—unless you want to create an opportunity to present an area you need an opening for. (More about this technique in the section, Follow His Lead—Your Way.) By sticking to the point, you will not force him to listen to a lot of things he has no interest in or put him in the position of having to interrupt you. You also convince him you are a person who is able to pay attention. On the other hand, if you fail to stick to the point, you risk giving the impression of being light-headed and disorganized.

Another caution about being talkative is to keep the length of your answers appropriate. Don't run on forever answering some question which could be answered adequately in a few words. On the other hand, if you are asked about your education or something substantial like that, give a real answer, don't just say, "It was O.K."

TALK ABOUT THE INTERVIEWER'S INTERESTS

Most of the time you should be talking about what the interviewer is interested in. This means listening to his questions, requesting clarification if they are unclear, and asking what he would like to know, if he is not giving you adequate indications.

There is an exception to this rule, a major one. It occurs when there is something important you want to tell the interviewer, but he is not giving you an opportunity. We will talk more about this under Taking the Interview Where You Want It to Go.

FOLLOW HIS CUES

Don't just listen to what the interviewer says and then proceed without checking with him. He may not be saying what he means. He may be inconsistent. He may not know himself. You might have misconstrued his intent. Perhaps you are giving him what he asked for, but he does not like what you are saying. Pay attention to the involuntary cues he is throwing out, as you learned to do in the last chapter—his facial expressions, the way he is sitting, whether or not his legs are crossed, and so on.

When you get positive cues, it is a sign that you are doing something right. Figure out what he is responding positively to and continue to develop it. It will usually be obvious, but if it is not, try to get some indications. A simple approach is just to stop talking for a few minutes and give him a chance to go on. Usually he will pick up on whatever it is that he is interested in. Or try asking him a few leading questions, along the lines of "Does that sound like the sort of thing you are looking for in an applicant?"

On the other hand, if you begin to get negative cues from him, stop talking about what you are talking about and stop relating the way you are relating. Try to figure out what is going wrong. It may be that you are simply talking about something he is not interested in. You may be revealing things toward which he is negatively disposed. Or you could be relating to him in a way he finds distasteful.

If the problem is not immediately apparent, investigate. What are you talking about, how are you relating, what are you trying to convince the interviewer of? Ask yourself if there is any aspect of the proceedings he might find objectionable. Then test your hypothesis by changing whatever element you think is to blame. Are his responses toward you improving? If they are, you have hit on the weak spot, and you have learned something as well. Make a mental note of his negative response, and think about it later. Perhaps it represents something you will want to rework in your P-Image.

If you can't get a sense of what is going wrong, your best strategy is to change the subject radically. Move on to a different area. Stop talking about yourself and ask him questions about the company—anything to get out of hot water.

CHECK WITH HIM FREQUENTLY

Following the interviewer's cues is simply a way of checking with him to see if you are on a successful course. Another way of checking with him is simply to ask a straightforward question: "Is that what you want to know?" "Would you like to hear more?" "How do you feel about that?"

But don't interrupt, contradict, disagree, or argue with him. Just don't. It's not worth taking the chance of alienating him.

TAKING THE INTERVIEW WHERE YOU WANT IT TO GO

Up to now we have talked about principles of responsive interviewing: how to answer questions, follow cues, be likable, and so on. Now the time has come to consider a more delicate subject —taking the interview where you want it to go.

When you are taking the interview where you want it to go, your basic task is to guide the interviewer's interest so that you seem to be responding to him, rather than the other way around. This should be done subtly. You must not give the interviewer the idea that it is you, rather than he, who is actually manipulating the interview.

FOLLOW HIS LEAD—YOUR WAY

One of the simplest ways to get the interview around to providing an opportunity for what you want to say is simply to follow the interviewer's lead—your way. This means that instead of answering his questions in the precise sense he means them, you use them as an opening to say what you want. For instance, suppose the interviewer has asked if you feel confident taking on a job as welfare worker that requires you to make visits in a somewhat dangerous area. You can answer briefly, or you can use the opportunity to highlight some aspects of your background that will reinforce the impression of your suitability for the job.

Sometimes, after the interview is well under way, you will learn things about a job that make you wish you had slanted your self-presentation differently. Use this technique to take advantage of any additional information the interviewer might willingly or unwillingly reveal.

This technique will also apply when you don't have precisely the sort of experience required by the job, but you want to interject a description of some related experience you feel is impressive enough to influence the interviewer toward greater flexibility. In this case you might offer this alternate experience as if you felt it fitted the bill, even though you know it really doesn't. If it shows you in a sufficiently attractive light, it might have a strong enough positive effect to counterbalance your formal shortcomings.

A caution is in order here. Don't overuse this technique. If you do, it can create a sense of frustration in the interviewer and a feeling that you are not hearing him. Use it once or twice at most in one interview and really make it count.

USE TEASERS

A more sophisticated and effective approach to creating openings for what you want to say is to first get the interviewer interested in the subject on which you wish to expound. One time-honored way of doing this is to use teasers.

Teasers are techniques which confidence men developed in order to involve people in their schemes without engaging their suspicions. Typically, the con man will drop a reference to the fact that he is about to make a lot of money on something. He will do this in a way that makes him seem like an innocent, as though he could easily be taken advantage of. If the person he is trying to con, the mark, doesn't rise to this bait, he will move on to someone else. Sooner or later, however, someone will take the bait and ask for details. Then the con man will act reluctant. This reinforces the impression of his naïveté and further heightens the interest of the mark.

Finally, when pressed, he gives details of an opportunity so fabulous that the mark's mouth waters and he starts to fantasize ways of cutting himself in. At this point the game has virtually been won. The mark, believing he has discovered an innocent, is about to con him. The con man, now beyond suspicion, is able to manipulate the situation passively, simply by releasing information in response to the mark's demands.

Now of course I am not suggesting for a minute that you operate as a confidence man. All I am saying is that there is a great lesson in human nature to be learned from this ploy, and you can use it to help yourself get hired. People are motivated, for the most part, by their own desires. For that reason, the easiest way to manipulate them is through something they desire.

When you go for a job interview, you are in the position of wanting something from the interviewer. This puts you at a great psychological disadvantage. You have to convince him that you are of value. And he, aware of this, receives your efforts with suspicion and resistance.

In order to be really successful in an interview situation, you must find some way of escaping and, if possible, of reversing this one-down relationship. In a very real sense, this whole chapter has been concerned with that. Precise, factual self-documentation; conveying an air of success; essential equality; avoiding a position of need; looking upon the interview as a mutual investigation—all these topics are addressed to the problem of transforming the one-down situation, escaping a psychological disadvantage, and allaying the interviewer's suspicion and resistance. Teasers take this process still further.

To use the technique of teasers, drop a passing reference to something about yourself which, you have reason to believe, the interviewer will perceive as having unusual value. Furthermore, mention it in a way that suggests you are somewhat unaware of its worth. Then wait for the interviewer to show interest. If he doesn't, forget it; you chose the wrong teaser. If he does, respond to his questions in an ingenuous manner, as if you are telling him about something you take for granted, not trying to impress him with an achievement.

The way this works is to allay his suspicions and to make him think of you as someone of value, someone he actively desires. Once you can accomplish this reversal and bring him to the point of actively pursuing you, you have attained psychological leverage, and the things you say about yourself will have a much more positive effect.

Let us say that you have been working on a new process which you know the company is interested in. You might mention that process in passing. Then, when the interviewer presses you for details, say as much as is appropriate about the process and your role in developing it, without seeming to attach undue importance to it. As the interviewer becomes involved, enlarge on your role in greater detail. However, avoid saying anything which might suggest that you are being disloyal to your previous employer, or that you are willing to give away company secrets, for this will give the impression that you are an untrustworthy person.

Your teaser will play on the interviewer's interest in you as a valuable commodity, and he will begin to want you in the company. When this happens, you will sense it immediately. All you need do now is to continue the conversation according to the guidelines set forth in this chapter, without seeming too eager. Then, if he takes the bait, you have a captive audience and you can proceed to develop your theme.

Again, be cautious when you use this technique. Don't overuse it, and watch for his cues. You should avoid taking the interview away from the interviewer. Make your point, then go back to his direction.

This chapter has covered the major skills necessary to talking about yourself effectively in the interview situation. At this point you should be almost ready to try an actual interview. First, however, you need some preparation for those less-than-straightforward situations which almost invariably arise. These are the traps interviewers set to trick you into revealing things about yourself, personal or professional, which might show you to be "unsuitable" in their eyes. Without mastering this material, you will find that many interviews go inexplicably awry, for reasons you will never understand.

TRAPS
INTERVIEWERS
SET
15

Every interviewer who is worth his salt is a master at setting traps. To understand why he does this, think of interviewing as a game. Your fundamental aim in this game is to make a positive impression and get hired. The interviewer's aim, on the other hand, is to trick you into revealing yourself, so that he can see through the impression you are trying to make and discover who you really are.

Thus interviewers do not approach you with an open mind. On the contrary, they have very specific ideas of what they are looking for, and they want people who fit them. These ideas begin with the Employer's Dream (you read about this in chapter 6) and are further defined by the specific requirements of the job, by the characteristic needs of the firm and the industry in general, by the mores of the region, and by the employer's personal biases. This means that although it is your aim to make a good impression, only the interviewer knows fully what will impress him. Unfortunately, this makes it a game where the interviewer plays with a closed hand and you play with an open one. This, as you know, is a good way to lose.

The simplest technique an interviewer has for finding out if you are the kind of person he is looking for is to ask you about yourself. But there is a problem inherent in this procedure. If you want the job, you are going to try to tell him what he wants to hear. The only way he can feel confident that you are not misrepresenting yourself will be if you don't know what he is after. So he will try to devise ways of drawing you out, without revealing what he is looking for, in order to find out whether or not you really conform to his Employer's Dream.

He will do this by asking loaded questions. These are questions which lead you to reveal yourself on key issues but do not reveal by their form or content what the issues are. Loaded questions are traps, and it is very easy for the unwary applicant to fall into them.

Your game is to catch these loaded questions, recognize the underlying issues, figure out what the interviewer is looking for, and represent yourself as that kind of person. If you can achieve this without his catching on to what you are doing, or if you just happen to be the right kind of person, you will be in a highly competitive position for the job in question. (Again, assuming you have the formal qualifications.) But if you fail at assuring him that you are what he is looking for, or if he suspects you of tricking him, you most certainly won't get the job.

The remainder of this chapter will show you how to recognize loaded questions and teach you some strategies which will not only keep you from being shot down but, in many cases, will turn the barrel back toward the interviewer.

TYPES OF LOADED QUESTIONS

There are basically two types of loaded questions which interviewers use—close-ended and open-ended ones. There is also a variant of the open-ended question which doesn't seem like a question at all. This is the conversational gambit. Let us look at each of these in turn.

CLOSE-ENDED QUESTIONS

Close-ended questions are really yes/no, true/false, and multiple choice, except that the answers you are to choose from are usually left implicit or unstated. When an interviewer asks you a close-ended question, it will probably sound as though he wants to find out about you in a general sense and is open to any reply you might give him. But there is a good chance that he has a "right" answer in mind. Giving it to him will be a hit in your average; not giving it to him will be a strike. Here are some typical close-ended questions.

- Do you like to travel?
- Are you engaged?
- How many children do you plan to have?
- Are you planning to go back to school?
- Why did you leave your last job?
- Are you out of the city much?
- How do you feel about working under a man (woman, person younger/older than yourself)?
- How do you feel about taking responsibility?

Most of these questions are of the yes/no variety, but some, such as "Why did you leave your last job?", are really multiple choice, although they might not always seem to be. For instance, although there are numerous stories you might give for having left your previous job, all of them will fit into one of a few categories the interviewer has in mind, such as "fired," "looking for something better," etc.

It takes only a little common sense to guess that most of the categories in his mind will be unfavorable. This is true even if you present extenuating circumstances that make it look as if it wasn't your fault. Thus, if you say you were fired but it was because of cutbacks, or the boss's son got the job, this will look better than being fired for incompetence, drunkenness, or rifling the till. But the question will still arise as to why it was you and not somebody else who got the ax. So it is always better to say that you left of your own accord because you needed more challenge and growth.

Upon first examination, you might not believe that common and innocuous-seeming inquiries like these close-ended questions are all loaded and that a wrong answer to one of them might disqualify you. Yet it is true. Each question listed is frequently used to get at information concerning things that companies have preset biases or personnel policies about, which you would normally have no way of knowing.

The following exercise will help you to understand the way close-ended questions work.

1. Write a complete and candid answer to each of the preceding close-ended questions.

2. Reread the Employer's Dream in chapter 6.

3. Ask yourself: If the company you were being interviewed by adhered to the Employer's Dream, would the answer you gave to these questions be acceptable or unacceptable? Could it be either? Why?

4. If you decide that an answer you gave either would have been unacceptable or could have been either acceptable or unacceptable, change or refine the answer to make it definitely acceptable.

Before beginning, study the following example. Question: "How do you feel about taking orders?"

1. *Candid answer:* "Oh, I have no trouble at all taking orders. In fact, I prefer functioning in a job with well-defined responsibilities."

2. *Reread the Employer's Dream,* paying particular attention to the parts relating to giving and taking orders.

3. *Analysis of answer:* This answer could be taken either positively or negatively, depending on the needs of the employer. The Employer's Dream suggests you show a willingness to take orders and function within the structure of the job, but it also emphasizes the importance of ambition, independence, and will-

ingness to take responsibility and supervise others. If the job called for someone who was to remain permanently in a position which called for the mechanical execution of company policies, this would be an effective answer. On the other hand, if the job required taking responsibility or led to a position of that nature, the answer might make you seem inadequate.

4. *Change or refine the answer.* Let us assume for the sake of the example that the position will eventually require taking responsibility for others and that therefore the answer would be inadequate. Its opposite would be something like: "I don't much care for taking orders, I would rather be in a position to give them." This clearly is also an unacceptable response, violating both common sense and the Employer's Dream. More suitable would be an answer which covers both possibilities and excludes neither. Something like: "I realize the necessity of taking orders if a business is to function effectively, and I am perfectly happy to do so. At the same time, I feel that I am a competent person, able to make intelligent decisions and accept responsibility, and I would welcome the opportunity to function in a supervisory capacity when that becomes appropriate."

OPEN-ENDED QUESTIONS

The second kind of question you will encounter in interviews is the open-ended question. Open-ended questions are designed to draw you out in a way which gives the interviewer an idea of the sort of person you are. Where close-ended questions are a fairly direct attempt to check you out on a particular issue, open-ended ones are much less specific, and the interviewer is more open to what you have to say. Nevertheless, open-ended questions are seldom as open as they seem. The interviewer will typically have a general area he wants to investigate. It might be something he can't ask about directly, because that would tip you off to what he is looking for, enabling you to tell him what he wants to hear. So he will ask an open-ended question, hoping to lead you to reveal those things about yourself he wants to know. Following are some typical open-ended questions an interviewer might ask.

- How do you feel about living in New York City (or wherever the job is located)?
- What sorts of things do you like to do in your spare time?
- How do you feel about ecology (the energy crisis, the election, or some other political issue)?
- How do you feel about homosexuality (women's liberation, or another current social issue)?
- What are your favorite sports (hobbies, books, magazines, plays, etc.)?

These friendly and seemingly innocuous inquiries could easily be as loaded as close-ended questions. A thoughtless response to any one might disqualify you.

This simple exercise will increase your understanding of loaded open-ended questions and show you how to deal with them.

1. Answer all (or as many as you like) of the preceding questions completely candidly. Write your answers.

2. Review the Employer's Dream, particularly the parts that seem relevant to these questions.

3. Analyze your answers from the viewpoint of the Employer's Dream. Do they show you in a favorable, unfavorable, or mixed light?

4. If an answer shows you in an unfavorable or mixed light, revise it to make you appear more acceptable.

5. Compare your revised answer to related parts of your P-Image. Does it suggest some way in which your P-Image could be further refined? If so, do it now.

Before you begin, consider the following example. Question: "The air in the city seems to be worse than ever today. Have you noticed it?"

1. *Candid answer:* "Yes. It's so bad I can barely stand to breathe. Sometimes when it's like this I have fantasies of blowing up the Con Edison plant, or else I just want to escape to Vermont or an island someplace."

2. *Review the Employer's Dream.*

3. *Analysis of answer:* Three strikes and you're out! It's obvious from this answer that you tend to be a malcontent, that you have infantile destructive fantasies toward authority, and that you are a bad risk in terms of staying on the job for a long period of time.

4. *Revise the answer.* A better answer would be something like: "I know, it is pretty bad. Still, it seems that recent environmental legislation is beginning to have a beneficial effect, and I expect there will be continuing improvement. Besides, I feel that urban life offers enough benefits to warrant some inconveniences." An answer like this would indicate that, although you are sensitive to your surroundings and their shortcomings, you are moderate, you believe in effecting change through established channels, and you are still essentially satisfied with the conditions of your life.

The Conversational Gambit

A variant of the open-ended question you will frequently run into is the conversational gambit. This is not a question but simply a topic of conversation that the interviewer casually brings up, like: "I was just reading the *Times* editorial on the new budget cuts." Conversational gambits are meant to draw you out on a particular subject. You can deal with them the same way you deal with open-ended questions.

IDENTIFYING LOADED QUESTIONS

There is no certain way of identifying loaded questions. However, the nature of job interviewing is such that any question not visibly and directly relevant to job qualifications might very well be loaded. For this reason, follow this first precept of indirect interviewing: *Whenever the relevance of a particular question is not obviously related to the job for which you are applying, assume that it is a loaded question.*

Does this mean that every general question an interviewer asks is loaded? No. On the other hand, he will be evaluating all the things you say and do and drawing conclusions about your suitability from them.

"But," you might object, "if I consider every question to be loaded, I'll constantly be watching myself and I won't be able to act natural."

Don't worry about that. You're not expected to act natural. You're interviewing for a job, not relaxing with friends. The interviewer expects you to try to be your most impressive, poised and well prepared. No matter how you behave, he will assume that it is at least in part an act, and your best act at that. So make sure it *is* your best act.

Since any general question might be loaded, and you are under constant evaluation, caution is your most appropriate attitude. No matter what you say, you should first try to hear it in your mind from the employer's viewpoint.

Loaded questions will probably, but not necessarily, stand out from questions that are being asked for their own sake. Beware of:

1. *Questions that seem personal rather than professional.*
2. *Questions about anything unrelated to job qualifications.*
3. *A line of questioning with an objective that seems vague, obscure, or irrelevant.*
4. *Questions that try to pin you down on an irrelevant issue.*

5. *Questions that seem out of the general context or flow of the conversation.*

6. *Questions given more or less importance than their content would seem to merit.*

As you can see, there are no hard and fast rules for identifying loaded questions, only general guidelines. The most important thing to remember is that you must cultivate a wary attitude toward all questions and conversational gambits. Keep in mind that even if specific questions are not loaded, you are being examined.

The six basic guidelines for identifying loaded questions have one common denominator. The loaded question will often stand out or strike a wrong note in the conversation. This is because it is dropped in for a special purpose and is only disguised to seem as if it flows out of the conversation. If you listen receptively and trust your intuition, you will find that you are able to pick it up.

If a question feels wrong, assume it is loaded and answer according to the strategies discussed in the rest of this chapter.

RESPONDING TO LOADED QUESTIONS

COPING WITH CLOSE-ENDED QUESTIONS

Close-ended questions sound as if they relate to you, but they are really concerned with the fulfillment of the Employer's Dream. As an example, let's take a seemingly innocuous and friendly question which might be asked of any childless married man or woman applying for a job: "Do you plan to have a family?" Some of us, uninformed of the biases in the average Employer's Dream, would probably gush on for a few minutes about how much we love children, dogs, and all helpless things and how we plan to have a big family, thinking we had discovered an area as safe and uncontroversial as Mom's apple pie, and as good for scoring brownie points. Nothing, however, could be further from the truth. On the other hand, a person who didn't plan a family might very likely admit it without a second thought. This, too, could be an error under certain conditions, depending on your age, your sex, the level and requirements of the job, and whether you will be working in an urban area where people's private lives are their own or in a company town where executives socialize.

Your plans for a family are a primary factor in deciding whether or not you are the *right sort of person* to hire. A young married woman who planned to have children would be considered a very bad risk for any job where turnover is undesirable or where substantial effort would have to be put into training her. This, of course, effectively excludes such women from all but the most routine and uninteresting sorts of work and sometimes even makes it difficult to get clerical and secretarial jobs.

However, let us consider the case of a young married woman who claimed that she did not want children. First of all, this claim would be looked on with suspicion, since employers believe that all young married women want children. Secondly, to the degree that she was believed, she might be looked on as unnatural, a bad risk, and—if it were a company town—unsuitable to socialize with other executive families, most of whom would have children. In fact, if you are a married woman at the age where you might still be expected to have children, there is almost no way to be fully acceptable to the average employer for any responsible job. Probably the best strategy is to manufacture some external circumstance which would make it seem that despite your wishes, you are prevented from having children.

On the other hand, a young married man who contemplated having children would be considered stable and an excellent risk. The exception, of course, would be any job involving a good deal of travel or frequent changes of location. The employer might anticipate that family demands would soon spur him to look for a more settled position.

Finally, a young married man who didn't plan to have children might be considered possibly unstable but socially acceptable in an urban job but socially unacceptable in the suburbs. He would be favored for jobs that require a lot of travel or frequent changes of location.

With this introduction we begin to see the problems posed by loaded close-ended questions. Now let us consider some ways of dealing with them.

The basic strategy for coping with close-ended questions is to figure out what the interviewer wants to hear. There are several steps in going about this.

Start with the Employer's Dream. Unless you have some real evidence to the contrary, you should always assume that every interviewer is looking for this. (Even if a particular one is not, he is highly unlikely to reject it.) So ask yourself how the question he is asking fits into the Employer's Dream. Let us stay with the question "Do you plan to have a family?" Obviously, it relates to the factors of stability, responsibility, heterosexuality, and social acceptability, among others.

Determine how those factors relate to you. As we have already seen, wanting children spells job stability for a man, instability for a woman.

Consider any special characteristics of the job: the company, the industry, the area, the kind of work, the setting, involvement with the public, special hours, travel, stresses, relationships with co-workers, special personality traits you will need for fields such as selling, detail work, or creative work. This will be easier if you have previously worked in the same field or a related one.

Then ask yourself, If I were hiring someone for a job with these special characteristics, what sort of people would I look for, and what sort would I avoid?

Finally, take into account any additional information you may have about the predispositions of this employer: the kind of company it is, the conditions prevailing in the business, and any personal cues from the sorts of people you meet in the office, the way the interviewer dresses, the furniture and decor, the magazines in the waiting room—anything and everything that would provide some idea of the predispositions of this employer. Ask yourself what attitudes seem to prevail and what sort of people they are likely to be looking for.

Putting all this information together, you should be able to guess what the particular company's dream of the perfect employee would be. Then you can cook up a reassuring response to almost anything you might be asked.

Prethinking

At first, recognizing loaded questions and figuring out what the employer wants to hear may look very complicated. Actually, it is mostly common sense.

It is also much easier in person than it seems on paper. If you have faithfully carried out the assignments thus far, you will be familiar with the Employer's Dream, and you will have constructed your P-Image. Just by projecting your P-Image, you will automatically satisfy most loaded questions, even if you don't pick them up. All that remains is to consider who a specific employer really is, how his dream differs from the general one, and what particular requirements the job in question might have. Then decide how these considerations apply to you. If you do this, you will find that you click right into place with what the interviewer is looking for.

However, do not wait until you are actually being interviewed to start examining these considerations. Prethink each interview thoroughly. Find out as much as you can about the job in advance, and then go through the four stages of preparation I have outlined as well as you can with the information at your disposal *before the interview.*

WHAT TO DO WHEN YOU CAN'T FIGURE OUT WHAT AN INTERVIEWER WANTS

The Counter Question

Most of the time, your new awareness that traps are being set will enable you to make a very educated guess about what an interviewer is fishing for with a particular question. Inevitably, however, there will be questions which you suspect are loaded, yet you will have no inkling of what the interviewer is getting at or wants to hear. When this happens, you need to follow a different strategy.

Consider this question: "Do you ski?" Here is a question that seems so innocuous and irrelevant only a paranoid would suspect it of being loaded, and only a psychic would know how to answer it if it were. However, let us say, for the sake of exposition, that your intuition is to treat it as a loaded question.

You have nothing to go on, but you can always ask, "Do you have some particular feelings about skiers?" If you are lucky, the interviewer might respond by telling you what he is driving at, giving you the opportunity to come up with a reassuring answer. However, there are some dangers to this direct approach. The first is that you might put an interviewer off this way. After all, he is being indirect for a reason, and even though asking him to show his cards could save you from a serious misstep, it might make him defensive. Furthermore, your answer will have less power to make a good impression since he will have given the game away. Another danger in asking directly is that the interviewer might simply lie.

Sometimes an indirect approach is more successful. Consider the following option.

Interviewer: "Do you ski?"

You (as if interested in the interviewer): "Oh, are you a skier?"

This variant will be less threatening to the interviewer because it looks as if you are responding to him, not trying to dope out the question. Then, if this ploy elicits any answer at all, you will be in a better position to make an educated guess about what he is getting at. For instance, if he replies, "Me? The only snow I go near is the kind you spray on a Christmas tree," you can feel fairly sure that the question about skiing was loaded, not asked out of general interest, and a negative answer is in order.

There will be times when you will have no choice but to ask or answer blind. In these situations it is better to ask, because you might have as much as a fifty-fifty chance of disqualifying yourself with every blind answer to a loaded close-ended question.

The Noncommittal Answer

An alternative strategy to the counter question, and often a far better one, is the noncommittal answer. Instead of asking the interviewer what he is getting at, find a way of answering which doesn't commit you. For instance, to the question, "Do you ski?", try an answer like: "I've done a little skiing." This answer could really mean you tried out for the Olympics but dropped out because of a hangnail and decided to go into insurance sales instead. Or, "I've often considered trying a little skiing." This might be another way of saying that you live in a basement apartment because looking down from a first-floor window gives you vertigo.

Once you answer ambiguously, he will often give himself away. If he doesn't, you can inquire gently, "Why do you ask?", which might elicit something more definite like, "We have a company ski program. We think it builds great morale and solidarity. It was one of the first things I instituted as personnel director." To which you can counter with something like, "Wow! That's just what I'm looking for."

On the other hand, if he says, "The last section manager was a skier, the first to leave on Friday afternoons and the last to come in Monday mornings. The other three days as well. We finally had to let him go." You can advance, "I know skiing does take a lot of time. That's why I've never gotten heavily into it. I've always been too involved in my work."

COPING WITH OPEN-ENDED QUESTIONS

As we have seen, open-ended questions, like close-ended ones, are intended to trick you into revealing things that can be used to judge you. The interviewer uses open-ended questions when he wants to know something about you but cannot ask directly, because if you see what he is getting at you will know how to answer. Through this stratagem he hopes to give you so much rope you will hang yourself.

Broad Questions

There are two types of loaded open-ended questions. The first is extremely broad and is designed to get a general sense of you. In this type the interviewer is looking for information which might reveal your suitability in a general area—personal, social, political, or the like. If you, like the average person, have a fair number of idiosyncrasies, you could easily disqualify yourself by carelessly answering open-ended questions of this sort. Consider the following somewhat tongue-in-cheek examples:

Interviewer: What do you like to do in your spare time?

Applicant: I spend a lot of time in the country.

Interviewer: Really? That's nice. Hiking?

Applicant: Mostly collecting rattlesnakes snakes for my collection.

Interviewer *(thinking): Weirdo. Reject.*

Interviewer: What do you do in your spare time?

Applicant: I spend most of my spare time doing volunteer work for Blooey.

Interviewer	*(interested):* Blooey? Don't think I've ever heard of it.
Applicant	*(with a sudden surge of animation):* Haven't you? Why, I can't believe that. It's the newsletter for ACNES—you know, Anarchists for a Completely New Start. *(He pulls out a copy featuring a cover story on the Bombers Convention held in the abandoned 18th Street subway station, with his byline.)*
Interviewer	*(to himself):* Troublemaker. Reject.

When you are asked open-ended questions like these, it is difficult to know exactly what to reveal and what to conceal. The basic steps in figuring out what the interviewer wants to hear, presented on the previous pages, are just as applicable to open-ended questions as they are to close-ended ones. Once again, you begin with the Employer's Dream and your P-Image. If you are a liberal Republican or a conservative Democrat, and your favorite spare-time activities are golf, tennis, and theatergoing, you know by now that you can probably talk about these aspects of yourself fairly candidly. But if you have discovered some parts of your makeup that are very far from the Employer's Dream, you had best use some caution in answering open-ended questions which take you into these areas.

You can get further guidance for what would constitute an acceptable answer to open-ended questions in a given situation by observing the norms which seem to prevail in the company, the industry, and the region. For instance, sales organizations, manufacturers' organizations, and advertising agencies all have very different expectations of the people they hire. A casual art department where women wear jeans and men sport beards and open shirts will be more tolerant of individuality than the customer service section of a third-generation Wall Street firm.

Narrow Questions

A second type of open-ended question you will encounter will be more narrowly focused: "How long have you lived in New York City?" By this time you will have no trouble guessing that this question, like the close-ended question, "Do you plan to have a family?", is probably aimed at guessing how stable you are and how long you are likely to remain with the firm. However, while the close-ended question "How long have you lived in New York?" is looking for an answer like "Ten years," this question is an attempt to elicit general information which will enable the interviewer to make a broader judgment. Single answers are less likely to lead to your rejection. Rather, it is the pattern which emerges that will gradually reveal to the interviewer whether or not you are the sort of person he is looking for.

The defensive interviewing techniques you are learning from this book will put you in a position in which you, rather than the interviewer, control the interview. However, maintaining this control and utilizing it for the purpose of getting hired will only be possible if the interviewer remains completely unaware of what you are doing. As long as he has not caught on, you will be able to second-guess him at almost every point, and by taking advantage of his prejudices and preconceptions you will turn his traps into opportunities for you to reassure and impress him. However, the moment he suspects what you are doing, the game is lost. The entire interview will be invalidated, and he will almost certainly reject you as a candidate for the job. That is why you must use every precaution to keep him unaware of what you are doing.

When you are asked a question such as how long you have lived in New York, and you realize it is aimed at determining your stability, it will be a temptation to answer in a way that indicates your awareness. For example, "Don't worry, I'll probably stay with Amalgamated until I retire." Answers like this are a great mistake. They reveal the game you are playing, and they will make the interviewer extremely uncomfortable both with himself and with you. For this reason, a basic rule of defensive interviewing is the following: *Always answer loaded questions without revealing that you understand what the interviewer is really getting at.*

The best approach to questions of this nature is to allow yourself to be led, as the interviewer intends, into a conversation that reveals what he wants to know about you. Of course, you must make sure that you only reveal what you want him to know. The following example provides a model.

Interviewer: How long have you lived in New York?

Applicant: Almost two years. *(Goes on in a conversational tone as if just reminded of it.)* I've really come to feel that New York is my home now. I couldn't imagine living anyplace else.

Or you could wait a while and then say something like, "I'm looking for a company to grow with so I can become a real part of it." In this way you will be reassuring him very directly, and he won't realize you have understood his question.

Counter Questions

Open-ended questions can often be turned even further to your advantage by converting them into counter questions.

Interviewer: How long have you lived in New York?

Applicant: About two years. By the way, are you just interested in someone to fill this particular slot, or are you looking for people to develop for high-level management positions?

Interviewer: We're always on the lookout for top executive talent that can move up in the company.

Applicant: That's good for me, because I'm really looking for a company that offers room for growth.

In this way, you not only will have answered the interviewer's question in the affirmative, but you will have given him the strongest possible assurance, the assurance that you wouldn't want the job if it were not right for you. This will put you in a very strong position in the interviewer's eyes. In fact, its effect will probably be immediately discernible in a warmer, less cautious attitude toward you.

DEVELOP AND PRACTICE YOUR OWN STRATEGIES

The strategies I have shown you for responding to loaded questions are basic and effective, but they are not the only ones possible. As you gain practice at taking interviews, in real life, in a workshop, or working at home with a friend, you will discover strategies of your own. Don't be afraid to use them. There is only one caution. *Get feedback.* If you are in a practice situation, ask the person interviewing you whether he or she picked up on the strategy and what effect it had. If you are in an actual interviewing situation, watch the interviewer. See what you can learn from him. Then, when you get home, try the new technique out on your practice partner, and see what you both think about it.

In job-targeting workshops we practice dealing with loaded questions in mock interviews. You can do this on your own with the help of a friend, and it will be a great help to you. Explain the kind of job you are looking for and have him or her prepare by reading this chapter and chapter 6, Employer's Dream. Then ask your partner to step into the employer's shoes and interview you. A friend who is in the same field would be best, because this brings more experience to the role of employer. However, even someone completely unfamiliar with the field will be able to do a surprisingly good job. You can help by filling in what you know about the things that employers in your field are looking for, and this will be an excellent refresher for you as well.

After the interview, ask your partner for feedback on how he or she perceived you in general, what made a good or bad impression, and whether your strategies were apparent. Practice like this until you are skilled at the strategies and are able to make a uniformly good impression on the interviewer. It would be even better to get more than one person to work with you in this way. Best of all, form a small group of friends who are interested in developing the same skills and work faithfully from the book with them.

BASIC STRATEGIES SUMMARIZED

1. *Whenever you do not understand how a given question relates to the job qualifications, assume that it is a loaded question. Beyond that, keep in mind that everything you say will be thought about, and be cautious.*

2. *By thinking ahead as much as possible, figure out what this particular employer's version of the Employer's Dream is likely to be. Decide how you and your situation fit into it. Then adapt your P-Image to the dream and work from it faithfully. Don't let a friendly interviewer mislead you into abandoning your P-Image and presenting yourself openly.*

3. *Try to figure out what close-ended questions are getting at. If you can't, either ask directly or indirectly or answer noncommittally. Never answer a close-ended question blind!*

4. *When you decide what the close-ended question is getting at, answer it positively. If you first answered noncommittally, commit yourself. If you have not yet answered, answer now.*

5. *When answering open-ended questions, stay with your P-Image, try to figure out what the interviewer wants to hear, and do not reveal that you have discovered the concealed question.*

6. *Answer open-ended questions with questions of your own whenever possible.*

NOW
THAT THEY WANT
YOU

16

Now you're coming into the home stretch. You have examined your career, located appropriate jobs, researched them, targeted your P-Image, and mastered skills of résumé writing, body language, and interviewing. Here you are, sitting in the interviewer's office, perhaps for the second or third interview, talking about a job you want so bad you can taste it, and seeing in his face the unmistakable signs of interest. Two hurdles remain: closing and then negotiating the best possible deal for yourself.

There is an ideal order for the closing and negotiating. First get the job offer, then negotiate. Do not accept the job until the amount of compensation has been settled. The reasons for this will become apparent in the following pages.

CLOSING

Let us start by considering the process of closing. Many books on how to get a job approach the problem of closing as if it is a task of salesmanship, to be pulled off almost by tricking the interviewer into hiring you. While this approach is not completely invalid—some techniques do help—there is one thing it tends to ignore. *Before any closing techniques can be effective at all, the interviewer must want you.* You cannot get a job through a closing technique. You can only bring the situation to a head that way. The interviewer's desire for your services is the lever that makes closing techniques work. Without it they either have no effect or, worse, a reverse one.

Daniel Beekman's Fear-Greed Hypothesis

One of the most trenchant analyses of the dynamics of job getting was given to me by Daniel Beekman. He calls it the Fear-Greed Hypothesis. The employer, not unlike most of humanity, is motivated by two principal emotions, fear and greed. The greed, in this case, is to acquire the employee who is best able to transform his operation into a more efficient profit center, and to do it at the lowest possible cost. The fear is that he is going to be duped into hiring an incompetent or a charlatan instead. Your task in getting hired is to allay his fears and appeal to his greed. Nowhere is this principle more central than in the closing process.

REASSURANCE TECHNIQUES

In keeping with the Fear-Greed Hypothesis, your first job is to allay the employer's fears and convert his defensive attitude into an acquisitive one.

To do this, you must establish the premise that the employer wants you as much as you want the job and that he has to win you over. You should approach the situation from four underlying assumptions which reassure the interviewer that you are not trying to get anything from him and that, in fact, he would be lucky to have you.

Assumption 1: You don't need the job! The best way to convey this, if you are already employed, is to suggest that while your present job is not optimal, it is satisfactory. When you are in between jobs, convince him that (1) you are not under pressure, either financial or psychological, (2) your being between jobs is purely a matter of choice, and (3) you have a number of options, job offers, etc., that you are considering, but you are still looking because you haven't found the right one.

Assumption 2: You would never take a job you are not enthusiastic about, and do not feel fully confident to handle, and are not committed to staying with. This assumption follows naturally from the first one, because there is no reason to take a job you are not enthusiastic about if you are not under pressure. To establish this assumption, never press or plead for a job or show desperation.

The process of interviewing the interviewer, which was discussed previously in chapter 14, is an important one with many applications. It enables you to get information about the job and the company which you can then use to excellent advantage on successive interviews. (Nobody ever remembers what information they have already divulged, and if, in the second interview, everything you say sounds right, they will not remember that they told it to you in the first one.)

Another application of this procedure is to allow you to control the interview. For instance, whenever you are in a tight spot and you want to change the subject, you can do it by interviewing the interviewer. Simply ask him a question about the company, the job, or the industry, preferably one that is difficult or challenging. In addition to making you appear intelligent and discriminating, it will distract him, involve him in formulating an answer, and frequently put him on the defensive. This is such a good trick that you should have a dozen or so of these sixty-four-dollar questions prepared in advance, so that you can spring them when the going gets tough and you don't have time to think.

The basic premise of interviewing the interviewer, as we have said before, is that you want to find out as much about the job and the company as possible in order to make the most informed choice. Any questions to this effect will be well taken and will have the desired effect of making you seem like you are a person who is extremely discriminating and who has to be convinced to join the company.

Assumption 3. You are enthusiastic about the company and most everyone in it, starting with the interviewer. You do not, of course, show this enthusiasm immediately, because it would be unbelievable. Instead, let it develop as the interview proceeds. Let the interviewer see you in the process of turning on to the things he is telling you. This will have a very salutory effect. When the second interview rolls around, you should let it be known that it is what you are discovering about the company that is bringing you back.

Assumption 4. If you decide the job is right for you, you will be hired for it. There are no tricks to establishing this assumption except for one—*believe it!* Assume it is true. If you do this, it will alter the entire course of the interview. You will respond in different ways, ask different questions, convey different vibrations, and in every way convey that you are a desirable candidate.

CLOSING BY OVERCOMING OBJECTIONS

Once you have established the four assumptions that serve to reassure the interviewer, you will move on to what is perhaps the most basic closing technique, overcoming the interviewer's objections to hiring you.

Since interviewers are putting their judgment on the line when they hire someone, all sorts of objections tend to develop in their minds. You need to overcome them. The applicant who is most successful at this will have the best chance of getting the job, all other things being equal.

Before you can overcome these objections, you must be able to identify them. The way to do this is through questions like "What do you feel stands in the way of a positive decision?" or "Are there any problems you see at the moment which I can help you clear up?"

The interviewer may then answer, "Well, I wonder whether

you have enough direct-mail experience to really fill this job."
Then, when you know his objection, you can formulate an answer
to reassure him.

Each time you identify and overcome one of these objections, you come closer to getting the job offer. So it is very
important to be persistent. Sometimes you will encounter a series
of objections to hiring you, yet you will be able to overcome all
of them and get the job.

There are times, however, when this technique will not
work. The interviewer's objections will be vague and ill-for-
mulated, he will be hard to pin down, and your answers will not
really satisfy him in any conclusive way. This is a bad sign. It
indicates either that he is unsure of what he wants or that he has
some serious objection to you that he is not willing to reveal,
because it is basically discriminatory, irrational, or personal. Either way, you are very likely wasting your time. He is probably not
going to hire you no matter what you do. So you should politely
extricate yourself from the interview as soon as you can and then
move on to the next opportunity.

MOVING IN ON SMALL POINTS

As the interviewing proceeds successfully and you come closer to
being offered the job, something strange is going to take place in
the interviewer's mind. It is called *the approach-avoidance phenomenon,* and it is a manifestation of the Fear-Greed Hypothesis.
Approach-avoidance is the psychological term for a situation in
which an organism, in this case the interviewer, is relating to
something, in this case you, that it both desires and fears. As the
organism approaches the sought-after object, fear increases to the
point where it overwhelms desire. Then the organism retreats to
a point where the fear lessens to a tolerable degree. At this distant
point, desire grows greater once again, and soon, warily, the organism begins another approach. An organism caught in this approach-avoidance cycle can continue this way almost indefinitely,

never quite getting there and never quite getting away.

How does this work in the interview? If you are targeting properly, you will become increasingly attractive to the interviewer. Soon he will approach the point of offering you the job. However, as he does this, his fears of making a mistake will begin to loom larger, and these fears will lead him to procrastinate and find all sorts of reasons why he shouldn't hire you. This is the crucial point in the interview. If you let him linger long enough in this scary place at the edge of a decision, he will begin to retreat again and may even begin considering another candidate or think about moving somebody up from within the company (thus lessening his fear of the unknown). On the other hand, if you try to force him into a decision through direct confrontation, you may panic him into a retreat.

While he is at this point, though, two things will be happening. One part of his mind, the frightened part, will express its fear of hiring you by raising a series of objections. Meanwhile, the part of his mind that is enthusiastic about you will already be trying to work out the details of hiring you and integrating you into the company. The interviewer will do a lot of this out loud, and through this process he will be providing you with *opportunities to close on.*

The interviewer's psychological process at this point is a twofold one, part approach and part avoidance. Therefore, your strategy must be twofold as well.

The first part of your strategy must deal with his tendency toward avoidance. You do this by continually identifying his objections to hiring you and overcoming them, as described earlier. Overcoming his objections will relieve his anxieties and move him closer to the point of offering you the job. Soon he will be ready for final closing techniques. This must not be a head-on confrontation of the "Well, how about it?" variety, because that might put him off. Just try a subtle maneuver designed to turn something that he wants to happen into something which has already taken place.

The right strategy here is to move in on small points. It is very simple and works like this. As the interviewer moves closer to the decision to offer you a job, he will begin to give you leads. He will say things like "Unfortunately, if you do come aboard, you will have to take an inside office until we take over the top floor in January" or "As you know, the job is not just getting out the newsletter, it includes a lot of fund-raising activities as well."

Leads like these are sure signs that he is already inwardly hiring you and is psychologically going over the logistics of fitting you in. This is the point at which you can begin to close.

The technique is simple. Take each of these tentative moves in the direction of an offer as if they are offers—and *accept them*. For instance, say, "That would be all right with me. I've suffered greater inconveniences than an inside office before, in order to accomplish something really important. I could be ready to start in three weeks if that would fit in with your schedule." Or, "That would be perfect, a heavy fund-raising tie-in would be just the challenge I'm looking for. I could spend the next few Saturdays familiarizing myself with the production routine and then slip in at the end of the month, if that suits you."

Is this technique always going to work? Not always. Sometimes you will be surprised to find the interviewer saying that the end of the month will be perfect and holding out his hand. But if he is not ready quite so soon, it doesn't matter. Having extended himself this far and being positively taken up on it, he will have begun to feel obligated to offer you the job. From here on in it will be easier going. He will continue to give you openings like the last one until he sells himself. Your job is to keep on accepting, up to the point where the job is offered to you. He may also go on raising objections during this period, but if you continue to meet them, the job offer will come soon enough.

A word to the wise here: Try to get the offer before you leave his office. All sorts of things can happen in even a week's time. People's enthusiasms cool, their fears increase, other applicants appear. Close quickly if you can. If you have gotten to the end of the interview and everything is going well, but you have still not arrived at an agreement, try to make it happen. Say something like, "It seems that we are close to an agreement, and I would like to go away from here with something positive. Tell me, is there something I can do to help you make up your mind?" It is best to push at this point.

TIGHTENING THE SCREWS

A point may come when everything seems right but you are still not getting the offer, and time is going by. This is where you can consider using a little pressure to force the employer's hand.

There is really only one way of putting pressure on a recalcitrant employer, and that is by considering another offer.

If you have been handling your interviews properly all along, he will already believe that you are considering other companies, other options, and even other offers. Now is the time for one of these offers to take on some added urgency.

The ploy goes like this. "Consolidated has made me an attractive offer. I promised that I would give them an answer by a week from Thursday. I would prefer to join you for all the reasons we discussed. But the Consolidated offer is an excellent one, and, frankly, I don't feel I can let it go by unless we come to an agreement."

Sometimes it will work, occasionally it will backfire. Don't use it unless you have to, but when you get to the point of diminishing returns in the interviewing process, this is your ace in the hole.

CONSENSUAL AGREEMENT

One more invaluable little closing trick. Perhaps you have come to the end of your third interview, and you are getting along famously. You have discussed and worked out everything from the location of your office to a five-year work strategy, and still no one has actually come out and said the words, "You're hired. Can you start on Monday?"

In a case like this, one thing you can do is assume that you have been hired. Simply proceed on the basis that you have the job and then make arrangements accordingly. For instance, say something like, "Well, I guess we've covered everything. I'm satisfied. Why don't I plan to come in about three weeks from Monday and get started?"

The worst the employer can do is say no. And all he has to do to hire you, if he wants to, is not disagree. If he lets you make the assumption, he is agreeing that you have the job.

This is a last-resort technique for reluctant closers. You can only use it when the interviews are far along and you sense that you really have the job, although the offer is not forthcoming. But if you find yourself in such a position, this can be an invaluable device.

NEGOTIATING

Now that you have finally been offered the job, the time has come to start talking about money. Negotiating for salary and compensation is a very emotional business. It is here that many people, after brilliantly pursuing and closing an opportunity, fall apart. They end up with thousands less than they could have gotten had they negotiated well.

To begin with, in many cases the employer is going to try to get you for as little as he can. He has several tools at his command that he will not hesitate to use to accomplish this.

His most powerful levers are your desire for the job and your uncertainty as to whether you have it or not. Because of this, the skilled interviewer will always try to open the subject of money before actually offering you the job. In this way he will try to manipulate you into thinking that the more reasonable you are about your demands, the better chance you will have of getting hired.

Resist this trick! Negotiations for salary must be limited to deciding on your compensation. They should never be allowed to dictate whether or not you will be offered the job.

PRINCIPLES OF NEGOTIATING

Your first principle in negotiating a salary is: *Never talk money until you have a firm offer.* If the interviewer raises the subject before then, tell him that you prefer to decide the basic issues first and not confuse them with salary negotiations. If he persists, tell him that you are sure you can reach a mutually satisfactory figure within the existing salary structure of the corporation, and then change the subject. Do not, if you can possibly help it, get trapped into premature negotiations.

The second principle of negotiating is: *Never actually accept a job offer until the question of salary is settled.* In this way, you turn the tables on the interviewer. Having offered you a job, he can no longer play the game of implying that the offer is contingent on salary. Yet you, with a firm offer, can always lower your demands if you cannot get him to meet them.

By negotiating salary after the offer and before the acceptance, you create a situation in which the interviewer feels he has to bid high for you. This is far better for you than feeling you have to bid yourself low to get the job.

SETTING YOUR PRICE

If you go into the interview without really knowing what salary to demand, the interviewer will soon find out and try to use your uncertainty to hire you for less than you are worth. Therefore, you should always know what salary to shoot for before entering into negotiations.

The salary you first ask should always be higher than what you will settle for to allow for negotiation, but it should not be high enough to price you out of consideration. If your real target salary is appropriate, an increase of 10 to 20 percent for your opening figure will be about right.

The question then arises, How do you know what salary goal to set for yourself?

There are two basic grounds for deciding what your starting salary should be. One is your previous salary and the other is what the job, or a comparable one, is paid in that company. Naturally, the interviewer will try to establish the lower one as the standard, because it is most advantageous to him. You must accomplish the opposite.

For instance, let us say that your previous job was with a nonprofit organization, and your salary was correspondingly low. The employer will try to offer you a modest increase, probably in the range of 10 to 15 percent, implying that far more is to come. His rationale is that it is a fair amount more than your previous salary. You, on the other hand, must insist on being paid at least what your predecessor earned. Your rationale is that the previous job gave you invaluable training for this one, and since you already paid for that experience by working at a low salary, the new company should compensate you fully for your present degree of competence. After all, the reason you are moving to a profit-oriented company is to increase your earnings. People tend to hold cheaply what they buy cheaply, and by demanding ample compensation you will also be earning more respect.

The situation may also be reversed. You could be coming from a highly paid position to a company which, though more desirable to you in other ways, has lower salaries. In this situation, the employer will try to use the typical salaries in his company as the standard for setting yours, and you will have to fight to make your prior earnings that standard. Your task will be to persevere without seeming unreasonable, particularly if it is an employer that might have genuine difficulty in paying a high salary, such as a nonprofit organization or a new and struggling company. Point out that you would willingly work for less, but your own economic needs and fairness to your family make that impossible. On the other hand, if it is a profitable firm that is just trying to keep your salary down on general principles, fight for the top dollar you think you can command. Point out that they are hiring you because you are exceptional, so you expect them to make an exception to their general guidelines and pay you what you are worth. It might not work, but remember, since you have a firm offer, you can always settle for less.

When you are in this position of moving from a higher-paying company to a low-paying one, you may have to compromise and settle for only a nominal raise of a few hundred dollars. Do this if the job is worth it to you, but try not to take a salary reduction; it looks bad on your résumé. Make sure that the new job offers more responsibility and a better title so that you can justify your lack of a raise to a future employer.

TECHNIQUES OF NEGOTIATING

To begin with, if possible, always let the employer make the first offer. He may surprise you and offer more than you would dare ask. All you have to do then is come back with, "How about . . . ," stating a figure of about 10 percent more, and you've got it. On the other hand, if he starts with a very low figure, you should take a deep breath and say, "I was thinking of something around . . . ," and name your starting figure. Then be prepared for a long round of negotiations and perhaps some hard compromises.

The greatest difficulty in salary negotiations occurs when the parties are not really in the same ball park. If he offers $28,000 and you want $35,000, you have grounds for negotiation. The figure can settle someplace in the low thirties, and though both of you will have to stretch some, neither will lose face or be forced to move into an entirely different league. On the other hand, if you are thinking $40,000 and he is talking $19,000, you have an impossible situation. He would have to increase his offer 50 percent, and you would have to come down by 25 in order to find a mutually satisfactory meeting place—about $30,000. Not only would this much movement be unusual, it would be difficult for him to rationalize in terms of job budgets, and your willingness to compromise that much would actually make you appear suspect.

One of the main reasons for having the employer tender his offer first is to avoid this sort of situation. Then, if he really comes in way below the figure you have in mind, you have a chance to re-evaluate. The first thing you must do is decide quickly whether the figure you are aiming at is worth holding out for or is merely what you had hoped to get. If you are really determined to get that much, you have no choice but to put your cards on the table and then do the best you can with negotiations.

If you are willing to compromise, however, it is probably best to do some of that compromising silently, so that the figure you name is within the range of his offer. You will come off with far more dignity asking for $29,000 and then negotiating hard on the ground that, say, $27,000 is the minimum at which you can maintain your standard of living, than you will demanding $39,000 and then settling for $27,000, or even $29,000.

Arguing Dollars

When it comes down to dollars, there are five basic arguments you can use to bolster your demand for more money.

The first argument is that you are demanding what that job or job level at that company typically pays or, alternatively, what the last person to do the job was paid. This tack requires that you first ask the interviewer what the salary structure of the company is and/or what the last person to hold the job was paid. This is a legitimate question to ask, and he should answer it. In fact, if he refuses to answer, the company's salary policies might be irregular, a good thing to watch out for.

Of course, the job may be newly created. In this case you

should try to find out what existing jobs it is on a par with and establish its value that way. If this figure is adequate, you are in luck. If it is not, you are in the difficult but not impossible situation of explaining why you are worth more than somebody else in a similar position.

The second argument is that you expect a fair increase on what you were earning at your last job. Use this argument when your last job was a high-paying one and the company you are going to offers at least roughly comparable salaries. If you are going into a company or industry where the salaries are much lower, you can't expect to apply this principle fully. But you might use it to do a little better, either getting the job upgraded or bargaining for extra benefits. Find out where the give is, and try to get some extra compensation there. If you are going into a firm where salaries are much higher, of course you won't want to apply this principle.

The third argument is that the amount you are demanding is what you need to live on, and the difference between what you have named and what they are offering means far more to you than it does to them. You will do your best for them; in return, you expect a salary adequate enough to keep from being beset by financial anxieties and difficulties. This is an appeal that has a little emotional blackmail in it. Within reason, it makes it very hard for the employer to say no.

The fourth argument is that you have a better-paying offer elsewhere. You would, of course, prefer this job or company for a number of sterling reasons, but it would be unfair to your family to expect them to live on much less, just so you can take a job you would like better. This is an excellent argument if you really do have a better offer in the wings. However, it is tricky as a bluff. If the employer says, "I'm sorry, but this is all we can pay," it is harder (though by no means impossible) for you to come back and say, "I've changed my mind, I'll take the job after all."

The fifth argument, which is both strongest and weakest, is simply to state a figure and declare that this is what you are worth and this is what you want. It is as strong an argument as you are a candidate. If you are really in demand, and you have gotten their enthusiasm to a high pitch, you can name your price and forget everything else. But this approach can seem arrogant and may invite second thoughts.

Helping the Employer Pay Your Price

Perhaps the salary you are demanding is more than an employer feels justified in offering, yet he still wants to hire you. In situations like this, you can sometimes actually help him to hire you by discussing the situation with him. The technique is basically to overcome his objections, the same technique you used to get the job offer in the first place.

The process starts with a mutual exploration of the difficulties standing between you and the salary you want. The basic premises here are (1) that he would like to find a way of hiring you, (2) that your demands are not unreasonable, and (3) that he is willing to explore them with you.

The best place to start is his reason or excuse for not being able to meet your salary request. Let us say he tells you that the job in question is usually budgeted in the range of $22,000 to $29,000 and that new employees usually start at or near the bottom. You are requesting $30,000. To begin with, you might ask if there is not some way he could justify paying you the top of the scale. For instance, couldn't he count some related experience you have had? This, of course, might lead to a discussion of this experience, which is a good opportunity to further sell yourself.

Or you might suggest that the job be upgraded to the next level in the organization, so that you would come in at a higher pay scale. Another possibility is to see if there might be some extra responsibilities you could take on which would provide a rationale for paying you more. After you start, you can soon demand an assistant to help you with these. Still another possibility is to find out what the person you are replacing was being paid. Sometimes it will be nearly as much as you are looking for, and that is a fair rationale for paying you at least as much.

The key to this sort of discussion is to be cooperative and understanding. You are not bargaining or demanding, rather you are working along with someone who wants to pay you your salary but is having trouble finding a way to do so. Of course, this is not always the reality—in fact, it seldom is—but it is an excellent strategy. It takes advantage of the fact that employers rarely come out and say they simply don't want to pay that much. Instead, they tend to make excuses, sounding as if they would like to, but their hands are tied.

This bargaining strategy, then, is excellent both in cases where the employer genuinely wishes to find a formula for meeting your salary demands and where he is just trying to beat you down with a number of spurious excuses.

If you discuss the reasons why he cannot pay you what you want, one of two things will happen. Either he will balk and close up, indicating that he has no intention of raising the ante, in which case you will have to accept that you are in a take-it-or-leave-it situation, or he will try to work it out with you and the two of you will find a way to improve the compensation. If he is open about it and comes up in price substantially, it indicates that he is a very fair-minded employer. You should thus consider the job even more strongly, although it may entail more economic compromise than you had originally thought.

A Few More Points

When bargaining, never say that a demand is unnegotiable unless you really have no intention of negotiating it. If you do, and your demand is not met, you will leave yourself no bargaining room and will lose the job.

A high-base salary is your primary goal, in most cases. First of all it is the main determinant of rank, and second, nothing is as spendable as cash. Unless you are in a very high tax bracket, straight salary is more important than fringes. So get that settled before you talk about benefits.

There are two types of fringe benefits that can go with a job: standard benefits that accrue more or less equally to all employees, such as health insurance and vacation time, and the special negotiable benefits that only the more high-powered executives are in a position to demand, such as stock options and profit sharing.

Standard benefits are just that. They come with the company, and there is nothing to negotiate for. If you are reasonably young and healthy, forget about them and just concentrate on your salary and your future. If you are nearing retirement, and are looking for a safe corporate home for the rest of your career, they are important. But again, they come with the company, not the job, so check out the company first.

Negotiable benefits, on the other hand, are really a form of alternate compensation essentially designed to provide work incentives and tax shelters for more highly paid executives. They can be as important as straight salary, or even more so. But you should let some accountant advise you about their value. Realistically, they are worth their cash value plus what they save you in taxes. However, from the point of view of negotiating salary and benefits, you need only count them at their cash value.

Now you are ready to go out and fight for what you want.

SOME ADDITIONAL PROBLEMS YOU MIGHT HAVE

WOMEN
IN A
MAN'S WORLD
17

It is not difficult for women to get jobs. In fact, they make up a substantial portion of the labor force. The real trouble women have is in getting better-quality jobs and equal pay for equal work. Recent legislation on equal rights in employment and the efforts of the women's movement have greatly improved both opportunities and compensation for working women, but there is still an enormous gap between their opportunities and those open to men. Although targeting can do little to alleviate these inequities, it can make you more realistic about them and give you the best possible chance for personal success.

As complicated as the process of job getting is for men, it can be even more so for women. For one thing, women face more competition for higher-level jobs just because fewer high-level openings exist for them. For another, women are subject to forms of discrimination, both conscious and unconscious, that men are spared. The last thing is that the changing social attitudes toward women and the feminine role by both women and men introduce an additional set of pitfalls.

Among the first problems for a woman looking for a career job are the attitudes of the interviewer toward women employees in general.

In chapter 6 you read the Employer's Dream, thereby becoming sophisticated about the fears and desires of the typical employer. The Employer's Dream holds for all employees, including women. However, since employers have so many specific fears about hiring women, this chapter will present a version of the Employer's Dream that pertains only to women. If you familiarize yourself with it, you will be on much firmer ground in every step of the job-targeting process and you will almost always know what to do in interviewing situations.

However, before even looking at the Employer's Dream for women, it is essential to study the employer's fears about female employees.

THE EMPLOYER'S FEARS ABOUT WOMEN

·She will not be dedicated to the job. A woman only considers a job something to do or a way to make a living before she marries or, if married, while she waits to have children.

·She will not throw herself into her work the way a man will, pushing herself in crises and working extra hours when the situation calls for it.

·She is used to being spoon fed and having special treatment and will expect this at work.

·She will be too emotional. A woman becomes depressed and is easily discouraged when things don't go well, crumples under criticism instead of rising to it, bursts into tears in times of stress, and in general is not able to behave the way a businessman does.

·She will ignore deadlines.

·She will not be punctual, arriving late, leaving early, and taking long lunch hours. Also, she will tend to cut Fridays and Mondays.

·Women simply can't do as good a job as men can.

·Women are not aggressive enough to compete with men.

·On the other hand, businesswomen who are sufficiently

aggressive are also "butch," bitchy, sexless, castrating, and otherwise threatening and unpleasant.

•Women cannot fit into a male world, particularly in an all-male group like a sales or presentation team traveling together. They will add an element of sex and frivolity, on the one hand, while on the other making the men uncomfortable and constraining the locker-room atmosphere that sometimes prevails in such situations. They will also interfere with the sexist and sexual entertainments that are often part of deal closings.

•Women take jobs away from men.

•Male executives will be emotionally unable to manage women with the same rigor and authority they use to manage other men. On the other hand, women will be insubordinate and make them look bad as managers.

If these fears seem not only unfair but arbitrary, it is because they are. They are the irrational but inevitable objections put forth by men who, on a deeper level, are simply disturbed by the idea of working with women as equals. The roots of these feelings go back to early childhood, to "no girls allowed" clubhouses and baseball teams and admiration for all the male strongholds where the important things of the world were done: the armed forces, the fire department, their father's offices. Later on, in high school and college, where these feelings should have been dispelled, they were nurtured instead by all-male schools and, even more significantly, competitive athletics. It is no surprise that men who were serious athletes are the most uncomfortable about working with women and try hardest to keep them off the team.

The long-term solution to this problem, as the leaders of the women's movement will corroborate, is to change these formative institutions and open every aspect of American life to women, so that future generations grow up seeing that the power centers of the world need not be male strongholds and that Mommy is as important a person as Daddy.

For those of you who are struggling to build careers in a world which is just beginning to be touched by the new consciousness, however, there are no easy answers. You will have to recognize and understand the fears, biases, and inequities of most men and of the system which you are trying to join and rise in. And you will have to deal with the problems and obstacles you encounter in a flexible, skillful, and objective manner, sometimes acquiescing, sometimes fighting, sometimes flattering, and sometimes confronting.

The information and tools in this chapter, as well as the rest of the book, will help you to get an important job, and that in itself is a real contribution to improving the career options of all professional women. Once hired, if you do your job well, play the game of organizational politics effectively, and rise to a position of authority and power, you will be in a position to do even more. You will find a number of resources to help you in this process. Good books to guide women in advancing their careers are coming out, and women's centers offer workshops where one can get reinforcement and guidance. This book will only help you get a job. But that "only" is a necessary starting point.

THE EMPLOYER'S DREAM FOR WOMEN

The Employer's Dream holds for everybody, even women. But since employers have specific fears regarding women employees, they need specific kinds of reassurance.

The employer is looking for:

•A woman who will be fully committed to the job and her career, one who either has no romantic, marriage, or family commitments present or probable or who can establish, without a shadow of a doubt, that the commitment to her job is greater than her personal ones.

•A woman who is very conscientious about her work, precise about details, scrupulous about deadlines, and accurate with figures.

•A woman who takes the job, the company, and the profit picture as seriously as the employer does.

•A woman who is friendly, cheerful, spunky, resilient, and able to take pressure, someone who never breaks down and gets weepy, frazzled, or sarcastic.

•A woman who can deal with improper and sexist remarks and advances adroitly and humorously, without confrontation, anger, or upset; who will not disrupt the office or alienate either a colleague or a customer.

•A woman who will not get romantically or sexually involved with colleagues.

•A woman who is extremely ambitious, but who will not push to advance or fight to get into areas of the company which are viewed as male strongholds. In other words, a woman who is ambitious for the company but not for herself at the expense of the company.

•A woman who looks smart and is impeccable, authoritative, and professional but still feminine—not obviously sexy but yet not severe and sexless either.

•A woman with top credentials, a proven track record, and, if possible, an MBA from Harvard.

•A woman who is rigorously punctual and who will work overtime without expecting extra compensation for it.

•A woman who will be one of the boys in terms of work output and acceptance of working conditions. This does not mean that she will tell locker-room jokes, drink with the men, or use the men's room. It does mean that she will carry her own weight, not be sensitive, and require no special consideration.

•A woman who is assertive in performing her job but acquiescent to authority.

•A woman who will not threaten the boss or other men in the office but, rather, makes men feel sure of their authority.

•A woman who will subtly flatter the boss's ego.

•A woman who will not introduce elements of female outrage and women's lib into what everyone knows is frequently a sexist, discriminatory, and exploitative situation. Instead, one who accepts inequity with humor and grace while tactfully trying to do the best for herself within the existing structure.

•Finally, a woman who will enable her employer to sustain the fiction that he is being generous, fair, and liberal when he bestows upon her any portion of the rewards she earns.

SIZING UP THE INTERVIEWER

Most interviewers you encounter will be men. As you know, men differ enormously in their attitudes toward women, but the one expectation almost all male interviewers will have of women applicants is that they fulfill their beliefs about what women should be like. Some men will value glamour in women applicants, some girlishness, and others professionalism. Almost all will have a type in mind and will hold out for it.

One of the most important things to find out at the beginning of the interview or, even better, before the interview (so that you can dress appropriately) is what the interviewer's feelings about women are.

There are, in fact, several basic sexist biases that men have toward women, and each one has to be handled somewhat differently.

THE PLAYBOY BIAS

The most widely recognized, although not necessarily the most prevalent, sexist bias, is the playboy's. This kind of man looks upon women as sex objects, playthings, decorations, and status symbols. A man like this is primarily interested in glamourous or sexy women who will titillate him and make a big impression on other men. He wants to be treated subserviently and flirtatiously, because he is irresistible and all women are infatuated with him not because he gives them a job.

As an employer, this kind of man may pay you well at the

outset, but you will have little chance for advancement. He probably will not demand much of you aside from a lot of little favors and good secretarial skills. When he does give you responsible work to do, he, not you, will get the credit for it.

Obviously, if you are being interviewed by someone like this and you want the job; you should try to dress the part. This means clothing which, though still tailored and professional, is sexier and somewhat frivolous; a tighter, more revealing fit, deeper neckline and heavier makeup all carefully selected to be provocative but not obvious.

The way to appeal to an employer like this is complex: simultaneously competent, flirtatious, humorous, and deferential. The idea is to suggest that you are there for work but you are not unwilling to play, and that you are independent and quick-witted, but that these qualities will be at his service.

Obviously, this is not a recommendation that you go for jobs with interviewers like this. It is just a discussion of how you might go about it, should you want to. The question you really need to ask yourself is: Is this man my future boss or just someone who is interviewing me? If it is the former, beware. If it is the latter, try to meet whoever you would be working for.

Very occasionally, when you are interviewing for a small company, you may run into a much more extreme version of this situation. Here you will be interviewed by a man who is openly flirtatious and even suggestive. He may stare at your chest, make inappropriate remarks, and even, if you seem acquiescent, go so far as to make some physical contact with you. Obviously, this is a man who is looking for more than just an employee, and to play the game with him is more than an interviewing ploy, it is an agreement. Unless this is really what you want to do, keep away.

THE PATERNALISTIC BIAS

A less obvious form of sexism, but frequently encountered, is the paternalistic bias. The paternalistic employer regards all women as "girls." He will relate to you in a way that seems concerned and protective, but he probably will not take you seriously, offer you significant responsibility, or give you real credit and fair advancement to a highly paid competitive position.

His paternalism, however warm it may seem from the outside, is really a means of keeping you down and protecting his self-image. It is also intrinsically opportunistic. Men like this can be extremely dangerous to work for. If you have any doubts about your own competence or your equality with men or, for that matter, if you haven't fully worked out your need to please your own father, you can become seduced into being a paternalistic boss's assistant, the good little girl that he couldn't live without —underpaid, overworked, and unrecognized. This is a terrible and demoralizing dead end, but a surprising number of bright, motivated, but insecure women arrive at it.

This kind of man wants you to be warm, girlish, admiring, insecure, and grateful. He wants to show you everything and to judge and reward your work himself. He doesn't want you to be strong and independent. Although he is unlikely to approach you sexually or romantically, he is apt to be jealous, so it is best not to let him see that you have an active social and sexual life. If you are married, do not make him too aware of your husband. Men like this require a great deal of loyalty. Prepare yourself for many a graciously demanded late night or weekend of work which you will have no choice but to agree to. Should you fail to play the game like that, the honeymoon will soon be over and resentment will take its place.

THE WORK-AND-PLAY-DON'T-MIX BIAS

The least obvious sexist bias of all, this is even more discrimina-tory than the others. Yet if your appearance puts you outside the sex-object or girlish categories, an employer with this bias may offer your best chance for employment.

Employers with this bias are threatened by women or, rather, by their feelings about women. Consequently, they only hire women who are, by conventional standards, sexually undesirable and who relate in ways that are sexually neutral. Their rationale for this policy is that work and play, *i.e.*, sexuality, don't mix. But of course their real motivation is fear.

An employer like this, with his willingness to hire women he does not find sexually attractive, may seem nondiscriminatory, but that is a misconception. The bias just runs in a different direction. For if he perceives you as potentially sexual he will not hire you, no matter how qualified you are.

The way to get a job from an employer like this is obvious. Dress neutrally and severely and present yourself in a very friendly, straightforward way. One caution: Once you have the job, don't blossom, or you may find yourself losing it soon after-ward.

THE NONSEXIST INTERVIEWER

Yes, there are nonsexist men in this world, and some of them are employers and interviewers. A nonsexist man will judge you on how well you can do the job and how well you can fit into the company. He will not be professionally concerned with your per-sonal life, except in the way it relates to your potential stability. He will not expect you to relate to him in a way that gratifies his ego, and he will not worry about you as competition. On the other hand, he will probably take a no-nonsense attitude toward you as a worker and will expect more of you in terms of performance than a sexist man will.

This sort of man requires nothing more than a suitable background, competence, and hard work. Furthermore, he will let you advance at your own pace. He is the best type of employer.

HOW TO FIND OUT THE INTERVIEWER'S BIAS

Once you know your interviewer's bias, you will be able to target your approach to him, should you choose to. The trick is to find out his bias early enough in the game so that you can take full advantage of it.

Since dress is such an important part of image, and dress is the one thing that cannot be altered significantly once the interview has begun, it would help to find out as much as possible in advance what the interviewer considers proper dress. Unless you know other people at the company, there are only two ways you can find out the interviewer's bias before meeting him.

The first is through talking to him on the phone. Evaluate how he relates to you. Is he businesslike, friendly, officious, or high-handed? When you talk to a nonsexist man, you will have the feeling of being respected as a person regardless of sex, even on the telephone. A paternalistic man may be overly warm and encouraging, treating you like a child. A man biased against sexually attractive women might give you the sense of being negated or being treated as a fact rather than a person. A man with a playboy bias may make flirtatious, inappropriate conversation over the phone. Unfortunately, none of these indications is very reliable. Many men will not reveal much about themselves over the phone, and what they do reveal will be ambiguous. Still, you have to make the best of the information you have.

Fortunately there is another means of finding out an interviewer's bias, as effective and foolproof as the telephone method is inconclusive. It is simply to meet his secretary. Men who have the power to do their own hiring almost always have a secretary who reflects their preferences in women. One look at his secretary, and you will know what type he favors. Then you can present yourself accordingly.

Often, however, you will have no natural opportunity to meet his secretary before you meet the interviewer, and you will have to create some sort of pretext. One of the best is to call and request some material on the company from her, say you are in the neighborhood, and volunteer to pick it up instead of having it sent.

When all else fails, dress in a fairly conservative and neutral manner and contrive to make the appropriate impression through voice and manner, after the interviewer begins to reveal himself. Or you could try this trick. Carry with you a few accessories which could slant your basic dress in different directions. After introducing yourself to his secretary and sizing her up, hightail it off to the ladies' room and do the best you can with makeup, your hair, and accessories like jewelry or a scarf.

WHEN THE INTERVIEWER IS A WOMAN

Your impulse might be to feel relieved when your interviewer turns out to be a woman, because you think that she will be much fairer than a man. Unfortunately, however, this can turn out to be untrue. Interviews with other women present their own complications and can prove to be just as tricky as interviews with men.

Women Who Look for Others Like Themselves

To begin with, professional women tend to have strong ideas about other professional women, ideas based on who they are themselves. Some women strongly identify with the women's movement and will favor others with similar leanings. Some professional women, especially those who are older, will have made it before the advent of the women's movement and may be unsympathetic toward it. They may feel that they didn't suffer prejudice themselves or that they made it the hard way, and so can you. Still another type of woman may identify strongly with traditional sex roles.

Of course, not every person is so small-minded as to discriminate against others with dissimilar orientations, but far too many do. Furthermore, many people do favor those they identify with, and when you are looking for a job, you need all the help you can get. This suggests that you should try to understand the attitudes of the interviewer as a working woman and try to be seen by her as a kindred spirit.

Fortunately, you need not figure this out ahead of time. You will have plenty of chance during the interview to see where she stands by evaluating her style, dress, and remarks, as well as by directly questioning her.

The key to success is to be as restrained as possible at the beginning of the interview. Then, as you begin to get a sense of who the interviewer is, you can gradually open up in a way that implies you are of like mind. You want to avoid projecting a personality that she will be unsympathetic to, so you must not seem frivolous and girlish to a woman who is all work and seriousness, or radical and militant to a woman who is traditional, and so on.

In fact, you might try to make a direct personal appeal based on similarity or even admiration. Accomplished women take justifiable pride in their accomplishments, which makes them susceptible to flattery, so let them see that you are respectful or even admiring of their achievements.

An excellent way to convey this is to take an interest in the interviewer's career. Ask her how she achieved her present position. This will tell her that you find her career path appealing and that you are a like-minded individual. It might dispose her more favorably toward you.

Women Who View You as a Threat

Some women have fought fiercely for the position they now enjoy, and they see every other woman coming into the company as a potential threat. When you are being interviewed by such a woman, you may sense great hostility (although, on the other hand, she may be expert at concealing her hostility with cordiality). A woman like this will have a perverse reaction to you. That is, the more you demonstrate ability, competence, and assertiveness, the less open to you she will be.

Your only hope with such a woman is to convey that you are not a threat to her. There are two possible ways of doing this. The first is to suggest that you are too unassertive or untalented to be a threat. The second is to convince her that, as talented as you are, you would be her ally and underling at all times.

Should you happen to get the job and work for a woman like this, you will be in a difficult position—so difficult, in fact, that you probably should not take the job. If you find yourself in this plight, the best strategy is to try to move laterally within the company so that she is no longer your supervisor. Try to do this in a way which will not antagonize her, perhaps suggesting that you want to do a different kind of work, not that you want to work for someone else. She could be a dangerous foe.

"WHERE DO YOU SEE YOURSELF FIVE YEARS FROM NOW?"

This is the question most often asked in interviews of women. It reveals, more than other questions, the paramount fear of employers, the fear that after they have trained and developed you, you will get married and leave, get pregnant and leave, or follow your husband to a job on the other coast.

Your response to this question, and any others which might relate to your future, however peripherally, should be to reassure the employer that you are truly a career woman and that you have no intention of giving up your career for anything! If you keep this firmly in mind, you will be prepared to recognize and answer properly all related questions.

The indirect questions the employer might ask you to get at the basic issue may involve what your husband or fiancé does and what your attitudes toward marriage, children, and working mothers are. Be prepared to recognize questions like these for what they are and field them.

Even if the interviewer doesn't question you on this issue, he will want to know, and it is good to reassure him. One of the best opportunities for this is when he asks, "Do you have any questions about us?" Here you could ask such things as where the job you are applying for might lead within the structure of the company. This sort of question indicates that you are looking for a long-term career situation and not just a job to hold you over until marriage comes along.

DRESS

Twelve major companies recently participated in a survey testing different styles of dress for women in interviewing situations. The looks ranged from a two-piece suit with a skirt, a one-piece dress à la Diane von Furstenberg, a two-piece highly fashionable outfit, and a tailored pantsuit. The winner was the two-piece skirted suit. The one-piece dress came in second.

In his *Woman's Dress for Success Book,* John T. Molloy, on the basis of his research, advises that women should always wear a skirted suit on a job interview. He goes so far as to recommend particular color combinations and fabrics, including variations for different regions. His emphasis is on conservative combinations like gray and beige, navy and white, or beige and light blue. Tops should be solid unless you are short, in which case you can wear a vertical stripe. His book is an excellent reference if you are considering fairly straight corporate employment.

Another point that most employers seem to agree on is that blazers make an authoritative impression.

Some no-no's for the corporate image are loose hair that hangs down in your face, jangly jewelry, and the no-bra look. The emphasis should be on the crisp, the tailored; in jewelry, solid, sculptured, very simple, and fairly expensive pieces are best (not glittery-expensive but designer- or artifact-expensive).

Of course, these guidelines only hold for jobs where a more or less corporate image is in order. If you want to work in a boutique, a theatrical agency, an art gallery, or any other special situation, you will have to check out the prevailing image and target your appearance accordingly.

OBSTACLES YOU PUT IN YOUR OWN WAY

How do you feel about yourself professionally? Do you feel that you are potentially the equal of any man, or do you secretly doubt yourself? Are you prepared to compete, be assertive, and stand on the merits of your own work, or are you inwardly afraid of competition with men and of failure? Do you use your femininity to bargain for special treatment in the male world?

On the other hand, how do you feel about using your sex appeal and charm to manipulate men to your own advantage when necessary? After all, sex appeal and charm are valid resources which men won't hesitate to use on you. And no competitive advantage should be discarded in a cutthroat world.

Many women labor under real disadvantages in the corporate world because on the one hand they are afraid to fight it out with men and on the other hand they hesitate to use their femininity when that is called for. If you suspect that you have attitudes which are handicapping you, you might consider joining a women's group where you could bring those attitudes to consciousness and examine them. You will encounter enough obstacles to career success without erecting your own.

IT'S WHERE YOU END UP THAT COUNTS

This chapter started by saying that women have no trouble getting jobs; the problem is getting better-quality jobs. It is time to come back to this. Just what does a good job consist of? One answer to this question concerns the obvious considerations of salary, working conditions, title, responsibility, benefits, and the like. But another answer to this question, an equally important one, involves where you can be five years from now if you do your job well.

This question, not surprisingly, is far more important for women than for men, although it is not unimportant for men either. Still, unless a man is in a very peculiar situation or has something major working against him, if he is qualified and does good work he can expect reasonable advancement in almost any company. This is not true for women. There are some companies that promote men and women without discrimination, solely on the basis of merit, but they are few and far between.

In fact, the companies which don't so outnumber those which do that anyone who counsels you not to work for an employer who discriminates against women is virtually telling you to stay unemployed.

The important thing to know, however, is that although most companies discriminate, they don't do so equally or in the same way. Your task is to find the company with a form of discrimination you can live with.

THE WAYS COMPANIES DISCRIMINATE AGAINST WOMEN

· Not hiring or promoting any women to executive positions

· Putting women into middle management spots but not top management

· Putting women into supervisory positions but only those supervising other women

•Putting women into executive positions but not giving them full voice with male executives on important issues

•Putting women in executive positions on all levels, but in fairly small or token numbers, so that it is much less likely for a woman to get a promotion than a man

•Putting women in high-level positions but requiring three times the qualifications than those required for a man (this is true of almost all firms that make wide use of female executives)

•Promoting women to executive positions but paying them less than men who do equal work, usually far less

MAKING DISCRIMINATION WORK FOR YOU

If the company you have found practices none of these forms of discrimination, it is a wonderful company indeed. Chances are that any company you are interested in will be guilty of some or all of them to different degrees, and you will just have to work in a less than fair situation if you are going to work at all. The real question is, Which set of discriminatory practices will work for you?

This seems like a stupid question, but if you think it over you will see it is not. For instance, consider a company that advances women readily up to middle management but seldom further. If you are already in middle management, this will not be a good company for you, since it offers little chance for further advancement. On the other hand, if you are a junior executive or are trying to get beyond clerical work into management, it could be an excellent place for a couple of years. Then, after you go as far as you can, you can jump off to someplace else.

Let's take another example. Consider a company that is not averse to promoting women, so long as they can continue to exploit them. They will give you as much work as you can handle, perhaps even a title to match, but insist on paying you half as much as a man would get for the same work. Now, no one wants to spend a lifetime so poorly paid, but on the other hand, promotions and senior positions are murder to get and worth a fortune at the right place. Go as far as you can for a couple of years in a company like this. Then, when you are at the point where you hold a really significant job, find another company that will pay you fairly for doing the same thing. This is not as difficult as it seems. Promotion policies being what they are, there is a shortage of experienced women executives at upper levels, and companies are looking for highly qualified women if for no other reason than to protect themselves again the accusation that they are discriminatory.

Another example? Let's say that, as in the foregoing example, you have just jumped from an underpaid upper-echelon job to a similar job in another company at a much better salary. Now, this company had to go outside to hire because they only want token women executives and are not developing talent internally. Sound bad? Well, yes and no. It could be all the better for you. You will have little competition, and you could end up a token vice-president.

Giving the matter a little thought, you will see that almost all these discriminatory practices can be gotten around in a way that enables you to use the job as a stepping-stone to another that will not put the same obstacles in your way. This is what the career game is all about, anyway. Remember, as long as the form of discrimination the company practices is not an obstacle to you *at this time in your career,* you don't have to worry about it. When you get to the point where your advancement is being blocked, then it is time to get out. Who knows, by then company policies might even change.

RECOGNIZING PREJUDICES

This naturally brings up the issue of how you tell what the prejudices of a particular company are. Of course, the answer is, as always, research. Ask questions, talk to people in the company, nose around, use your eyes, look at the employee roster. And while you are at it, keep these basic questions in mind:

1. *What does the distribution of women in that company seem to be? Are they all clerical or on lower levels of management? Or are all managerial women confined to some operations and excluded from others?*

2. *Who is the highest-ranking woman in the company? Is she an exception, or are there others just below her? How long has she been in the company? Is she much better qualified than the men on her level? Is she as well paid and respected? Does she seem to enjoy comparable perks such as a good expense account, profit sharing, and a company car?*

3. *Do executive women supervise executive men? Or are there only other women reporting to them?*

4. *Is the salary distribution of the company equitable, so that women draw equal pay for equal work? Or do most of the women get less than most of the men?*

5. *Are most of the nonclerical women in the "assistant to" class? For example, are they assistant to Joe Oaks, the sales manager, rather than assistant sales manager? This "assistant to" position is the pits—all the work and nothing to show for it when it's time to go.*

6. *Are the executive women as visible as executive men? That is, do they work directly with customers, attend conventions, and represent the company at trade shows and in professional organizations and the like? Or do they stay behind the scenes, getting the work done, while men make public appearances? This is not just a matter of ego, because it is in these public performances that you make contacts that frequently lead to really desirable job offers.*

If you are seriously considering or being considered by a company, and if you have any choice in the matter, keep researching these questions. By the time you get to the point where you can answer them, you will know a lot about the company, probably far more than you would have wished to. You will be able to evaluate for yourself whether it can meet your needs or whether you should wait for the next offer to come along.

TO LIB OR NOT TO LIB

Over the last fifteen years, the women's liberation movement has greatly improved the lot of the working woman, changing attitudes of employers toward women and those of women toward work. Also, as a result of the movement, legislation has been enacted making job discrimination on the basis of sex illegal. Large employers throughout the country have all, to varying degrees, yielded to pressure and made positive changes in their hiring and promotion policies. Corporations have also learned to give lip service to the goals of the women's movement. Despite this progress, however, the movement and women who espouse it are still widely perceived within male corporate circles as something between a real pain and a real threat.

If you are politically active in some aspect of the women's movement, know that most employers who suspect the fact will fear you may create agitation within the company. Therefore, they will be prejudiced against you.

Despite this, a number of books advising women on their careers suggest confrontation tactics in dealing with interviewers who persist in asking potentially discriminatory questions. For example, Betty Lehan Harragan, author of the widely read *Games Mother Never Taught You*, offers the following advice:

> 1. Never answer out-of-bounds, irrelevant questions on written application forms. The blank spaces force the interviewer to invade your privacy face to face so at least you have a chance to play the game one-to-one.
>
> 2. Use "Ms." as a title to correspond to the innocuous "Mr." If pressed to reveal your marital status, answer single, because you

are looking for a single job and you will be singly responsible for your performance.

3. Questions about children are pertinent only if you will be bringing children to work with you. Respond to such questions by asking about their on-premise child care facilities. When you find out that none exist (as you inevitably will) answer no or zero to the question since its relevance to your possible job is exactly zero.

4. To lightly parry malicious queries about contraceptives, reproductive plans, cohabitation arrangements or living style . . . respond to such questions by professing interest in the topic and the patterns or trends noticed by the interviewer. The nature of your reply might be:

"How interesting that you asked about contraceptives. I've been doing some research myself. What forms do you find most popular with the employees of this company?"

or

"I've noticed that five of your questions have had a direct or indirect sexual focus. Would you mind reviewing the prerequisites you have in mind for me? I'm wondering if there's more here than meets the eye about the proposed job duties."

This form of parry is about as light as yelling "Pig!" and shooting a kick to his crotch and is likely to be about as successful at getting you the job. Harragan seems to anticipate this failure with equanimity as she counsels, "If these calculated moves to maintain proper direction of the job interview don't do the trick, get out of there fast, and not necessarily politely. If you are certain at the beginning that the company is a bad place for women to work, you can be sure you'll have no future there anyway." But unless you can walk away from the job with equal equanimity, you should think twice before you try these tactics.

I'm pretty much in agreement with Harragan when she says that women are subject to all sorts of discrimination in the corporate world, but I think her advice to women with corporate ambitions is dangerously misleading.

Up-against-the-wall responses, no matter how adroitly put,

will end your career before it gets started. The slightest hint of this sort of militancy will absolutely kill an interview, and a good interviewer will not even let you know it. He will be so sensitive to the possibility of being accused of discriminatory practices that he will appear to sympathize and accept your position, but you won't have the shadow of a chance of getting the job.

Not only that, you won't do anything to further equal opportunity either. You will simply reinforce the common but covertly held impression that liberated women are to be humored and kept at a distance and make the interviewer that much more determined to screen out all but the most acquiescent and exploitable females.

Nor does Harragan's suggestion, "If you are certain at the beginning that the company is a bad place for women to work, you can be sure you'll have no future there anyway," convince me. First of all, you are not sure at the beginning. That is why you are there. Second, just because the interviewer is a jerk, the company is not necessarily a lousy place for women to work, unless you will be working for the interviewer, which is only sometimes the case. And third, women have gotten ahead in business by fighting their way in, not by walking away. If you tell the interviewer to shove it, you are not going to do anybody any good, but if you successfully infiltrate the company, get a job you want, and rise to a position of power, you will be one more woman in a position to accomplish real changes.

All interviewers, even those who are far too careful or respectful to ask personal and potentially discriminatory questions, want to know enough about your private life to determine that you will be on the job for a while and not let them train you and then leave to get married, have children, hitchhike to Guatemala, or whatever. The real trick is not to refuse to answer these questions but, rather, to find ways of answering them without their being asked. Your goal should be to drop information about your personal life, as though innocent of its implication, that lets the interviewer infer that you are a stable career prospect. Say something like, "My husband and I have decided that children are not in line with the life-style we have chosen for ourselves." Or, "Now that our children are grown, I feel I can finally devote myself to the career I have always wanted."

This sort of unasked-for reassurance is, as we have already said, even more convincing than the asked-for kind and will go a long way toward getting you hired. Even if the interviewer realizes that you are telling him what he isn't permitted to ask, he will probably appreciate your making his job easier. (Of course, there is always the chance that he will be suspicious as well.)

There is another sort of reassurance that you should give the interviewer, and this is direct reassurance about your attitude toward women's lib. No interviewer wants to hire a militant, and he needs to be reassured that you are not one. This doesn't mean you should revert to the attitudes of the fifties. Most of the time, this will be totally unnecessary (though not always). But it does mean that your approach to woman's consciousness, though self-respecting and properly assertive of your rights, should not be threatening. Formulate your position carefully in advance and be able to express it in a few well-rehearsed sentences.

Find a way to introduce these sentences at some time during the interview. Say something like, "As a woman, I feel the best way to have my value recognized is to do the job as well as anyone possibly could." This will bring beams of approval to his face. No chip on your shoulder, no special treatment asked for, and a determination to really work.

Or, if you really have a strong stomach, you could try something like, "I feel that no intelligent company would discriminate against someone who demonstrates the ability to make a real contribution, just because she is a woman. It simply wouldn't be in their own interest." Incidentally, he himself, even if his company is the biggest hotbed of chauvinism on the block, probably fervently believes this.

Anyway, the message is clear. Disregard it at your own peril.

ONE OTHER THING

Some writers suggest that you can force an interviewer to give you a job by challenging him on his discriminatory practices and even bringing legal action to bear. This is always a possibility, and if you try it you will certainly discourage similar practices in the future (or at least encourage greater caution). However, this strategy, even if it gets you a job, is unlikely to further your career. Few companies where real executive careers are possible have a sufficiently cut-and-dried promotion policy to enable you to prove discrimination year after year. Also, any company you storm like this will devote untiring efforts toward keeping you down and making your life hell.

Furthermore, this approach is a long shot, and while you are fighting the case in court, you might not be working. You will be expending time and money which you are unlikely to be repaid. This kind of action is practical only for people whose aims are political rather than career-oriented, or for those women who feel a strong vocational pull toward traditionally male careers such as fireperson or tugboat captain and have no choice but to sling it out.

MAKING
TOKENISM WORK
FOR YOU
18

Prejudice in business, as in most things, is a fact of life. Women, people over forty, people with foreign accents, Jews, and all non-Caucasians will find that prejudice is fairly widespread when they look for a job. It is illegal, many of the most flagrant practices have stopped, there are now many opportunities, and where prejudice does exist there is on occasion recourse to the law. But despite all that, prejudice is something you have to be prepared for.

There are, of course, thousands of jobs where prejudice is not a problem: city, state, and federal civil service jobs; jobs in education; technical and service jobs in some industries and areas; lower-echelon management positions in garages, fast-food restaurants, and dry cleaners; and all democratic strongholds where either government standardization or the law of supply and demand ensure that any qualified person has a good chance. (Although even here, a nice clean-cut Ivy League type will usually beat you out, should he apply.) But the good jobs, the real plums, the inside spots that lead to wealth and power in corporate America—these jobs are different. They are mighty hard to come by, and they are carefully protected by multiple screening procedures, and the people who get them—the people who even hear of them —are the right color and come from the right background.

Nevertheless, antidiscriminatory laws and public opinion have pressured industries into making some token openings for minority-group members on executive levels. And, though minority executives, even in these rare positions, are frequently insulated from the real power and mobility by hidden political networks, it is possible for one to break in and, once in, to play his hand so well that he becomes known as O.K., wasp-like, skillful, discreet, diplomatic, extremely capable, reliable, and nonthreatening. Such a person, working within an organization which feels it should have some upper-echelon minority executives, can rise to a position of some eminence.

If, as a minority member, you restrict yourself to applying for positions that are totally nondiscriminatory, you really don't need this chapter, prejudice will not be an obstacle, and the targeting techniques in the rest of the book will be more than sufficient. However, if you are going to venture into the more dangerous but often more rewarding waters of corporate America, you had better first arm yourself with every tool you can.

ALL MEN ARE NOT EQUAL, AND ALL MINORITIES ARE NOT EQUAL EITHER

Who is a minority-group member and who is not? There are many ways to approach this question in the abstract—country of origin, first language, racial stock, and so on. In practice, the answer is much simpler. If you are white and do not have a foreign accent, you are not a minority member. Everyone else is.

This means that Parisian émigrés, southern blacks, second-generation New York Puerto Ricans, and physicists escaped from behind the Iron Curtain are all, in some sense, lumped together. They are all different, foreign, peculiar, and unknown; they are all subject to stereotypical prejudgment (the essence of prejudice), and they are all, or at least most, at a considerable disadvantage in the job world. But there the similarity between them ends, because if, in the eyes of the employer all men are not equal, neither are all minorities equally unequal. Crudely put, there are desirable minorities and there are undesirable minorities. Those who meet the most relentless forms of discrimination are blacks, Latin Americans, Filipinos, southern Italians, Greeks, and any other peoples who came here in large numbers to escape substandard economic and cultural living conditions at home.

However, this separation into desirable and undesirable minorities is a gross oversimplification. The truth is that each minority with which Americans have any degree of familiarity has a stereotype attached to it (in some instances, a range of stereotypes). Thus blacks are still widely felt to be hostile, shiftless, and lacking in intelligence. Japanese are considered rigid, literal-minded, punctual, precise, and excellent at electronics. And Frenchmen are believed to be refined, aloof, clever, and sexy. These characterizations might seem to be bad jokes, or throwbacks to an earlier era, but they actually still prevail to an alarming degree.

If you are a recognizable minority member, expect to be perceived in terms of the stereotype or stereotypes associated with your group, rather than as an individual with a given background and a set of skills or abilities. Whenever you target for a job, you must always be aware of this stereotype, for you will have to work within it, sometimes trying to overcome it and at other times actively taking advantage of it.

KNOW YOUR STEREOTYPE

This could be unpleasant but you have to do it, because it is essential to everything in this chapter: Find out precisely what stereotypes, in the broadest sense, are attached to your minority group.

Easy, you may say. I know that already. And you will proceed to reel off the characteristics you feel most people assign to your group. But do you really know, or are you being unrealistic? Are you being too kind to yourself on the one hand, or too hard on yourself on the other?

CHECK YOUR PERCEPTIONS

Just to be on the safe side, I suggest you check your perceptions. What do other members of your minority group think the stereotype consists of, particularly those with business experience? How is your minority group portrayed in popular literature? What common clichés are used to characterize it—such as, for Latins, "passionate, volatile, macho men who suppress women" or Scandinavians, "dour, phlegmatic people who pass the long winter nights in saunas, drinking, and commiting adultery and suicide"? How is your group portrayed in tasteless jokes? If you or your children are subject to overt prejudice, what sorts of things are you taunted with?

One of the best ways to investigate this matter is to enlist the help of nonminority friends. Convince them that you want neither protection nor ego stroking. Rather, you need the truth, as hard, brutal, and complex as it is, about what others really think of your people. Your informant will probably be able to tell you a great deal offhand, having soaked it up in the process of daily living. If he is willing, he can find out a great deal more just by talking to his family, friends, and, above all, business associates. "Hey, Ned, what do you think of Indians?" "India Indians?" "Yeah, think they're all like that? Think one of them could make it selling mutual funds? Only to other Indians? How come?" You will find out what you are up against soon enough.

SOME THINGS ALL STEREOTYPES HAVE IN COMMON

As I have said, some minority stereotypes are seen as undesirable and some as desirable, but none are all good or all bad. Every one has its positive and negative points. Furthermore, it is not always the relative degree of desirability which is most important but rather the particular traits involved. You must work with these traits when you are targeting. For instance, being labeled as precise or threatening or passionate may work to your advantage or disadvantage, depending on the situation.

So after you research your stereotype and find out as much as possible about it, the next step is to divide the stereotype into its primarily positive and negative traits. For instance, the positive stereotype for Japanese includes the traits of neatness, cleanliness, reliability, intelligence, and ability in engineering, mathematics, and technical areas. The negative stereotype includes clannishness, conformism, conservatism, lack of individual initiative, and inflexibility, as well as lack of imagination. This will give you a good idea of its strengths and weaknesses on the job market.

Next, identify those traits which might be seen either as positive or negative, depending on the employer. For instance, the cluster of conservatism, obedience, and lack of personal initiative that the Japanese stereotype offers may be extremely appealing to employers looking for people to slavishly but efficiently follow orders or carry out routine tasks (even high-level ones such as engineering). However, the same traits would not appeal to an advertising agency or a public relations firm.

It is important, then, to be aware of the ambiguities in your stereotype, so that you can exploit your potential strengths.

HOW DO POTENTIAL EMPLOYERS VIEW YOUR STEREOTYPE?

The next question to research, and this is a targeting task, is: How do the employers you are interested in view the particular traits which are part of your stereotype?

This task is essentially an extension of the work you did in chapter 7, Describing the Job. It is partly a matter of research and partly just thinking the thing through.

The thinking-through part requires considering the various

traits that make up your stereotype and asking yourself how the employer you have in mind will view each of them. Obviously, some traits, such as a violent temper or unreliability, will appeal to virtually no one. On the other hand, as already noted, traits such as conservatism or snobbishness have their market, albeit a specialized one.

Do the research systematically and carefully, so that you become aware of all your strengths and weaknesses, so far as a particular employer is concerned.

DEVISE A STRATEGY FOR TARGETING YOUR STEREOTYPE

Once you have gotten this far, the next step is to devise a strategy to counteract those traits which your desired employer might find objectionable and maximize the ones he might find attractive. Or, to be blunt, figure out how to come across as a "good type" within the range of possibilities that your group or stereotype offers.

In order to do this, we must look at the following areas separately: family background and education, job history, personality, personal image, and even body language.

YOUR FAMILY BACKGROUND AND EDUCATION

Americans are a very democratic people. But you will do much better in the corporate world if you come from the ruling elite of an undeveloped country than if you are pulling yourself up by your shoestrings from its peasantry or urban poor. So represent yourself as a member of a high social stratum if you can possibly pull it off. You can concoct many stories to account for job hunting in the United States rather than managing the family plantations or refinery. Some noble-sounding possibilities are, "I wanted to prove to myself that I could become a success on my own," or, even better, "I couldn't continue to live amid luxury, knowing my poor starving countrymen were paying for it with their blood and sweat." No matter that those poor, starving countrymen were actually your immediate family.

On the other hand, if you are an American black, give the idea that your father was a respected physician or professor in some genteel part of the South.

The idea is this: If you come from an underdeveloped country, your origins should be upper class. If you come from a developed country or are an American minority member, your origins should be middle class (or upper class for certain high-prestige jobs). Under no circumstances should you admit to working-class or peasant origins. Farming is an exception for American minority whites—providing it was a large farm, not fifty chickens, four hogs, and three acres of truck vegetables.

Carry this concept through as much as possible. You should not have grown up in the slums or fought your way up with your fists; that was for another era. Corporations want people they can be comfortable with, people who ate well and went to decent grammar schools.

Talk about your home values—books, baseball, honesty, self-reliance, hard work, and ambition.

When it comes to higher education, it is important for minority members to have attended good schools. If you are foreign educated, places like Cambridge or the Sorbonne have the right sound—even better if you were sent there because your family didn't want you educated in Caracas. "I was sent to Cambridge for undergraduate work and then went on to Stanford for my MBA," is just about perfection. Also, remember, it is much harder for an American company to check out transcripts in Paris than in Philly.

If you are an American-born minority, having gone to a prestigious school helps. If you have not done so, you will be excluded from many better jobs. Your best bet, in this case, is to get into a top university for an MA in some relevant area. It will give you the stamp of respectability faster than anything else you can do.

YOUR JOB HISTORY

If you are a minority applicant for a mainstream corporate job, the only jobs which will count in your favor are other mainstream jobs. Crossing over from industry to industry is possible and in some ways may be your best bet. If you can rise to a position of respectability and prominence in a less discriminatory area like public service, you will have a better chance of getting an upper corporate job than you will by working your way up from the mailroom.

Marginal jobs, however, particularly those such as manual labor, shopkeeping, lower-level work in service industries, or restaurant work, are taboo for a minority member. Jobs like these will just confirm the prejudice that minority members are best suited to menial jobs, and will brand you as someone who is unemployable in the corporate world.

So when you target your education, completely delete any mention of manual labor and menial or marginal work you may have done. It is better to lie flagrantly, and get found out on four out of five applications, in order to have a good chance on the fifth, than it is to allow yourself to be stigmatized in this way.

YOUR PERSONALITY

This is one of the most important areas of targeting for the minority applicant. You have already considered the stereotype that every potential employer will have of you and decided which aspects to overcome and which to try to take advantage of. The personality you project is one of the primary means you have at your disposal of accomplishing this.

Avoid Militancy

To begin with, heed these general warnings. Some minority groups are undergoing internal movements which include elements of militancy toward white Establishment America. If you have chosen to work in the mainstream, you have already decided that the militant path is not for you. Do not allow yourself to display the slightest nuance of militancy in attitude or behavior. Do not engage in political discussions in interviews. And, avoid like the plague anything in dress, hairstyle, or demeanor which might identify you with militant factions. If you feel guilty about this, make a financial contribution to the organization of your choice, see a therapist, or change direction and follow the dictates of your conscience, but don't think you can come across angry and make it in the white corporate world. You can't, and you will be wasting hard-won opportunities if you deceive yourself about this.

Another warning. Other minority attitudes exist which, though not militant, contain a sense of having been wronged and being owed special treatment by the world at large. Many times these feelings are extremely well founded. Nevertheless, do not share them with your work colleagues, and particularly do not reveal them to your interviewer. They suggest that you are an inferior and a malcontent, when what you really want is to reassure the interviewer that you have overcome any early disadvantages and are now, despite superficial differences of race and origin, fundamentally very much like him.

YOUR PERSONAL IMAGE

WHEN IN DOUBT, GO WASP. There are times, as we have already seen, when particular ethnic and personality traits will be to your advantage in job getting. However, much of the time this will not be clearly indicated. For this reason, a basic Ivy League WASP image is the most desirable one to convey. Exceptions to this might be in creative fields in more urban areas, where the look might be somewhat more hip, as in New York or Los Angeles. In this case, adjust your image accordingly, but try to stay on the more conservative side of what is acceptable.

Beyond this, we get into special cases where you must target your stereotype to the wants of the employer. Some examples will be the best way to approach what is required here.

Let us say that you belong to a minority whose stereotype contains elements of frivolity and laziness—Latin Americans or southern Italians, for instance. For most mainstream employers, you will want to combat this image as much as possible. Effect a precise, forceful, but level manner of speaking and wear Ivy League suits in conservative patterns, chalk stripes or tweeds. Have your hair a little more severely trimmed than your colleagues, don't sport a mustache, smile little, listen seriously, cultivate an attitude of thoughtfulness, even deliberateness, and learn to count to ten before you express an opinion.

On the other hand, if you are Japanese or German, your stereotype might suggest stolidity, lack of imagination, and excessive conservatism. You could try to combat this with a bright and relaxed manner, slightly longer hair, and more flamboyant and casual dress, particularly in your choice of accessories. A little overstatement is usually necessary to counteract the preconception.

Or, as a minority member, you may possess a trait which works in your favor. For instance, if you have a good French or northern Italian accent, it can be a great advantage in many luxury businesses, particularly those where you work with the public. Play that air of old-world sophistication to the hilt. A good upper-class British accent can be a tremendous advantage throughout the corporate world, suggesting erudition and cultivation to many Americans, but it could be a disadvantage in advertising, suggesting you are not attuned to the American mass consciousness.

There really are no guidelines here. You must understand

your stereotype and the wants of your employer and proceed accordingly. You might even find that your type has so many advantages in some industries, and so many disadvantages in others, that this will influence which field you choose.

Accent

In America, where background can be concealed, only two things make you a minority: the color of your skin and your accent. You can't change the color of your skin, but you can change your accent. The prestige accents are northern Italian, French, and British. Sometimes a slight Germanic one is O.K., at least in some industries; in others, even a northern Italian or French is not. The only consistently good accent is public-school British. All other non-American accents waver in effect between slightly undesirable and disastrous.

But that is not all. Even if you are American born, you may have an accent which will work against you. Remember, an accent is the way you sound when you are talking to people who did not grow up in the same place as you (this may be as small an area as a single neighborhood in Queens or a region in Appalachia).

Acceptable standard American speech has its roots in the Midwest, and it is the way people talk on TV. If you sound like this, you have it made. Many other accents are O.K., and others are O.K. in some places and not in others. Deep southern accents are unacceptable, except in the South. Light southern accents are O.K. for whites but not for blacks, who must speak impeccable standard English. Western and southwestern accents are pretty acceptable on the whole, as are most eastern accents. New York accents are bad news, except in New York and Los Angeles. Beyond this, every region has its slum, rural-poor, and urban-backwater accents, the distinctive intonations of which make a bad impression. New York City, for instance, features distinctive stigmatizing accents of the Bronx, Brooklyn, and Queens. Many other cities have similar phenomena, and rural areas also have distinctive accents which are to the speaker's disadvantage. Various minority groups frequently have distinctive accents which vary further from region to region. Most blacks speak with distinctive intonations, as do Latin Americans.

A good accent is one of your greatest assets. Regardless of color, if you have any accent other than a prestigious one, and you are trying to rise in the corporate world, get rid of it. It will be greatly to your disadvantage; it will keep you pegged as a minority person, an outsider. The way to do this is to go to a competent speech coach who specializes in this kind of work. (Theatrical ones are best.) Avoid university or night courses; you don't get the individual attention here that you need, and the instructor may have as strong a regional accent as you do, but courses like that are only good enough to get you civil-service employment.

Dress

Dress impeccably, dress conservatively, dress as "they" do. Avoid any ethnic overtones in your dress, any types of clothing commonly associated with your minority group. The only exceptions might be if you are trying to overcome a trait in your stereotype, so you choose accessories to make you look slightly less conservative or more serious, or if you are trying to reinforce a prestige ethnic image by wearing English hand-tailored suits. However, these are only minor variations. Basic dress should be the uniform of the industry you are working in or trying to get a job in.

BODY LANGUAGE

Body language—the way you stand, sit, walk, move, or use your hands when you talk; the expressions on your face, the distance you customarily establish between yourself and another, your degree of eye contact, your handshake, whether and how you embrace or otherwise touch men and women—all of these things are primary indications of your ethnicity. Along with dress and accent, they constitute the impression of your being foreign.

The principles which apply here are no different from those in the rest of this chapter. If you come from a high-prestige minority, your distinguishing body language will lend you an air of distinction that will be in your favor. If you come from a low-prestige minority, your distinctive body language will brand you as a "common" member of that minority and will work against you.

You can also use body language as a tool for emphasizing some personal traits and de-emphasizing others. For instance, if part of your minority-group stereotype is stolidity, you can overcome this by learning to use your hands, your facial expressions, and the inflections of your voice more expressively. If flamboyance and frivolity are among the undesirable traits, you can counteract them by adopting conservative body postures, limiting face and hand movements, and speaking in measured tones that rely more on language than inflection to make points.

Unfortunately, the creative use of body language is an extensive subject, one that is very hard to do justice to when you are limited to the written word. Even if there were space to cover it thoroughly here, it would be impossible to convey what you need to know to make the changes you might want to make. In an area such as this, training under a skilled coach or teacher is essential.

If you feel your body language is working against you, or if you would like to make creative use of it to change your image, it is imperative that you get professional help. A good acting coach of the classical kind has sufficient mastery over movement to show you how to convey the image of a ninety-year-old woman just by using your hands, for instance. Working with someone like this will be a time-consuming process and will not be inexpensive, but the results will be worth it if you are serious about a corporate career. Your goal is to learn to present yourself, in accent and body movements, in that standard middle-American fashion approximated by TV announcers. If you can master this, you will make a positive image everywhere you go.

The image portrayed in this chapter of corporate America as a prejudiced institution is an unpleasant one. And the stratagems suggested to facilitate rising in it are in some ways equally unpleasant. Furthermore, many of them require great perseverance for success. Nevertheless, they represent the only effective way of freeing yourself of a stereotyped minority image that may otherwise forever impede the growth of your career.

Obviously, only you can decide whether or not you want to take the extreme path of eradicating your ethnic characteristics in the ways outlined in this chapter. Not only is it difficult, it requires losing a real part of your identity. Further, it is in many ways a humiliating path to follow. However, it is the only really effective one. Since the early days of American history, this question of either assimilating into the mainstream culture or retaining ethnic and cultural characteristics has confronted minorities. It is to be hoped that as our society continues to mature, stratagems like this will be increasingly unnecessary. In the meantime, you have a right to try to play any role in society you choose. Assimilation will make one role, that of mainstream executive, more accessible.

INDEX

Abilities: demonstrations of, 98-99
  portfolio showing, 100-103
  selling your own, 94-103
  targeting of, 92-103
  tests of, 99-100
Accents, 248-50
Accomplishments: pleasure in, 159
  reviewing, exercise in, 149-50
  talking about, 148-57
Adjectives, avoiding, 151-52
Appearance, 108-10. *See also* Clothes
Approach-avoidance phenomenon,
  200-201
Aptitudes, 92-93
  testing, 93
Assertiveness, 157-58

Beekman, Daniel, Fear-Greed
  Hypothesis, 197, 200
Being liked, 106, 112-13
Being perceived as right kind of
  person, 111-12
Belief in yourself, 95, 158-59
Benefits, fringe and negotiable, 212
Blacks, 240, 241. *See also* Minority
  groups
  in Employer's Dream, 62
  family background and
    education, 244-46
  speech, 249, 250
  stereotypes, 241
Body language, 131-46
  composedness, 143
  direction of body, 141-42
  eye contact, 138
  facial expressions, 138
  feedback from, 144-45
  gestures, 139-41
  inclination of body, 141
  of interviewer, 139-45
  of minority groups, 250-51
  openness, 142
  parts and whole, 140-41
  pattern of whole body, 144
  posture, 135-36, 142-43
  practice in reading, 145-46

relaxation, 138-39
rhythm, 143

Careers: aptitude and potential for,
  92-93
  establishing yourself in, 15-18
  fulfillment in, 20-21
  growth in, 20
  healthy, signs of, 19-23
  organization of, 19
  questions on, 24-27
  success in, 21-22
  tasks in, 27
Closing techniques, 196-204
  approach-avoidance phenomenon
    in, 200-201
  overcoming of objections,
    199-200
  reassuring employer, 197-99
  strategy in final agreement,
    200-204
Clothes, 109-10
  differences between companies,
    52
  for minority group members,
    248, 250
  for women, 110, 221, 224, 225,
    228-29
Companies, 46-54
  corporations, 48
  dying industries, 22-23
  government agencies, 51
  healthy, 22-23
  individual differences between,
    52-54
  nonprofit, 49-51
  ownership of, 48-51
  privately owned, 48-49
  professional, 51
  research on jobs in, 66-67
  size of, 47
Counseling: and aptitude tests, 93
  and belief in yourself, 95

Dictionary of Occupational Titles,
  38

253

Dress. *See* Clothes

Education, 75-83
  analysis of your background,
    77-78
  in job descriptions, 64-65
  of minority group members,
    245-46
  pinpoint targeting, 80-83
  in résumé, 79, 120, 218
  and skills, 95-96
  targeted to Employer's Dream,
    78-80
Employee in Employer's Dream:
  ability, 59
  desirability, 61-62
  profitability, 61
  stability, 60-61
  suitability, 59-60
Employers: attitudes toward
    women, 216-18, 230-34, 237,
    238
  equal opportunity, 69
  "our kind," 69-70, 76
  selling your skills and abilities to,
    94-103
Employer's Dream, 55-62, 176-77
  education targeted to, 78-80
  employer's questions in, 58-62
  and job descriptions, 63-64, 70
  and loaded questions, 177,
    179-82, 184, 186-87, 191, 194
  women in, 60, 63, 216, 218-20
Enthusiasm, as job-hunting asset,
    159-61
Ethnic groups. *See* Minority groups
Experience: redescription of jobs,
    88-89
  reordering of priorities, 89-90
  retitling of jobs, 87-88
  selective deletion of jobs or tasks,
    90-91
  and skills, 92-93, 95-98
  subtitling, 88
  targeting your job history, 84-91
  See also Résumé
Eye contact, in job interviews, 138

Facial expressions, in job interviews,
    138
Family plans: questions on, 184-86
  of women, 185-86, 227-28,
    235-37
Fear-Greed Hypothesis, 197, 200
Fields of work, 41-45
  questions on, 43-45
Flirtatious behavior, in job
    interview, 139, 220-21
Fringe benefits, 212

Games Mother Never Taught You
  (Harragan), 234-36
Government agencies, 51

Harragan, Betty Lehan, 234-36
Hiring process: being liked, 106,
    112-13
  being right kind of person,
    105-6, 108
  closing, 196-204
  employer's decision, 107-8
  prescreening, 104-5
  qualifications for job, 107
  salary negotiations, 204-12
How to Get a Better Job Quicker
  (Payne), 149-50

Interviews: being liked in, 106,
    112-13
  body language in, 132-46
  as conversation, 168-71
  desperation or need in, 163-66
  essential equality in, 161-63
  following interviewer's lead—your
    way, 171-72
  in hiring, 106-8, 112-13
  job information from, 66-69
  as mutual investigation, 166
  overcoming objections, 68-69,
    199-200
  questions in, 176-95
  relating to interviewer, 161-71,
    198
  teasers in, 172-75
  telling about yourself, 147-75

traps set by interviewers, 176-95
  by women, 225-27
  of women, 220-38

Job descriptions, 38, 63-71
  abilities and skills in, 65
  educational requirements in,
    64-65
  and Employer's Dream, 63-64,
    69, 70
  personal requirements in, 69-71
  redescriptions, 88-89
  reordering of priorities, 89-90
  research on, 66-69
  retitling of jobs, 87-89
  selective deletion of jobs and
    tasks, 90-91
  subtitling, 89
  in targeting of experience, 84-91
  in targeting of skills and abilities,
    96-98
Jobs: finding new, 15-16
  help-wanted ads, 38
  listings of, 38
  personal image in getting, 104-13
  prescreening for, 104-5

Militancy: of minority groups, 247
  of women, 235-37
Minority groups, 239-52
  accents, 248-50
  body language, 250-51
  clothes, 248, 250
  desirable and undesirable,
    240-41
  in Employer's Dream, 62
  employment, 239-40
  personal image, 247-50
  prejudice against, 239-40
  stereotypes, 241-44, 248
  targeting of stereotypes, 244-52
    education, 245-46
    family background, 244-45
    job history, 246
    personality, 246-47
Molloy, John T., books on dress,
  109-10, 228

Negotiating for salary, 204-12
Nonprofit organizations, 49-51

Occupation analyzer, 31-40
Occupations: fields of, 41-45
  right, 28-40
  self-analysis and evaluation of,
    31-40
  wrong, 29-30

Payne, Richard A., 149-50
Personal image: appearance, 108-10
  being liked, 106, 112-13
  being perceived as right kind of
    person, 111-12
  and job requirements, 70
  of minority group members,
    247-50
  remaking, 70
  targeting, and getting jobs,
    104-13
Portfolios, 100-103
Positive Professional Image
  (P-Image), 12-13
  and loaded questions, 187, 191,
    195
  in résumé, 120, 124
  telling about yourself, 147-75
Posture (sitting), 135-38
  forward, 135, 136
  of interviewer, 141-43
  Lincolnesque, 135, 136
  relaxed, 135-36
Prescreening for jobs, 104-5
Professional identification, 110
Professionals, groups of, 51
Psychotherapy, 95

Questions: on accomplishments,
    149-50
  on careers, 23-27
  in Employer's Dream, 58-62
  on fields of work, 43-45
Questions in interviews, 176-95
  broad, 190-91
  close-ended, 178-80, 184-87
  conversational gambit, 182

Questions in interviews *(cont.)*
  counter questions, 188-89
  loaded, 177-87
  narrow, 192-94
  noncommittal answers, 189-90
  open-ended, 180-82, 190-95
  prethinking, 187
  strategies in dealing with, 194-95

References: checking, 107
  not included in résumé, 129
Résumé, 84, 86, 117-30
  combination, 120-22, 127-28
  cover letter, 117-19
  do's and don'ts for, 129-30
  education in, 79, 120, 128
  functional, 120-21, 125-27
  guides for, 130
  language of, 123
  reverse chronological, 120-25
  selective deletion in, 90-91
  targeting, 118
  for women, 129
Right kind of person: being
  perceived as, 111-12
  and family plans, 185-86
  in hiring process, 105-6, 108
  "our kind," 69-70, 76, 108

Salary negotiations, 204-12
  fringe and negotiable benefits, 212
Secretary: in interview, 132-33
  reflects employer's preference in
  women, 224, 225
Self-documentation exercises,
  154-57
Sitting posture. *See* Posture (sitting)
Skills: demonstrations of, 98-99
  portfolio showing, 100-103
  targeting of, 92-103
  tests of, 99-100
Stereotypes, 241-44, 248
  positive and negative, 242-43
  strategy for targeting, 244-52
Success, 21-22
  and assertiveness, 157-58
  and belief in yourself, 95, 158-59
  and enthusiasm, 159-61
  and liking your work, 159

Teasers in interviews, 172-75
Telling about yourself, 147-75
  accomplishments, 148-51
  avoiding adjectives, 151-52
  following interviewer's lead—
    your way, 171-72
  precise descriptions, 152-54
  relating to interviewer, 161-71
  self-documentation, exercises,
    154-56
  success conveyed in, 157-61
  teasers in interviews, 172-75
Tests: of abilities and skills, 99-100
  of aptitudes, 93
Tokenism, 239-40
Training and skills, 92-93, 95-98

White Anglo-Saxons (WASPS): in
  Employer's Dream, 62
  minority members, WASP-like,
    240, 247
Women, 215-38
  attitudes toward, 215-17
  clothes, 110, 221, 224, 225,
    228-29
  discrimination against, 230-38
  in Employer's Dream, 60, 63,
    216, 218-20
  employer's fears about, 216-18
  family plans, 185-86, 227-28,
    235-37
  feelings about themselves, 229
  interviews of, 220-27
    finding interviewer's bias,
      224-25
    nonsexist interviewers, 223-24
    paternalistic bias, 222
    playboy bias, 220-21
    women as interviewers, 225-27
    work-and-play-don't-mix bias,
      223
  legal action against
    discrimination, 238
  militancy, 235-37
  recognizing prejudices against,
    232-34
  résumés for, 129
Women's movement, 215, 225-26,
  234-37